WHAT EVERYONE IN BRITAIN
SHOULD KNOW ABOUT
THE POLICE

WHAT EVERYONE IN BRITAIN SHOULD KNOW ABOUT THE POLICE

David Wilson, John Ashton
and
Douglas Sharp

Blackstone Press

Published by
Blackstone Press Limited
Aldine Place
London
W12 8AA
United Kingdom

Sales enquiries and orders
Telephone: +44-(0)-20-8740-2277
Facsimile: +44-(0)-20-8743-2292
e-mail: sales@blackstone.demon.co.uk
website: www.blackstonepress.com

ISBN 1-84174-261-9
© David Wilson, John Ashton and Douglas Sharp 2001
First published 2001

British Library Cataloguing in Publication Data
A catalogue record for this book is available from the British Library

Typeset in 11/13pt Times by Montage Studios Limited, Tonbridge, Kent
Printed and bound in Great Britain by Antony Rowe Ltd,
Chippenham and Reading

Contents

Acknowledgements

The authors would like to thank the following people: Barbara McCalla who typed much of the manuscript; colleagues at UCE in Birmingham including John Rouse, Chris Painter, Chris Barnes and Kester Isaac-Henry; and colleagues on The Crime Squad, including Colin Savage, Dave Stanford, Sue Lawley, Bas Javid, Howard Groves and Jess Redford.

John Ashton would particularly like to thank Celia, Ellis and Rachel Ashton; Leslie, Lois and Eva Clifton and the Directors and staff of Just TV. Douglas Sharp would particularly like to thank Christina Sharp. David Wilson owes — as ever — a great deal of thanks to Anne Maguire.

Introduction

THE ROLE OF THE POLICE

In the first few days of March 1999, the Head of the Kenyan Police Force paid an official visit to Britain as a guest of the Foreign and Commonwealth Office. Commander Waiganjo was here to 'learn about how the UK police really work in general, and in an accountable and democratic society in particular', according to the press release of the Foreign and Commonwealth Office (*Guardian*, 5 March 1999). Ironically, the visit was to take place only days after the publication of a withering report about the murder of the black teenager Stephen Lawrence and the police investigation that had followed his death. The Macpherson Report (Macpherson, 1999) pulled no punches and was scathing about institutional racism within the British police force in general and the Metropolitan Police in particular, who were to be Commander Waiganjo's hosts during his stay.

We know nothing of Commander Waiganjo's views about what he observed, but his visit reminds us that for many people in other countries (and indeed in our own) the UK police remain 'the best in the World'. As such they are a model to be copied by those nations who want to adopt a style of policing which is consensual rather than confrontational, and which seeks to serve rather than dominate the community. These would be lessons that Commander Waiganjo would have done well to absorb, given that Kenya is a dictatorship and that he is most associated with Kenya's notorious and repressive riot squad, the GSU.

Yet international comparisons cannot disguise the fact that the Macpherson Report, like the Scarman Report after the Brixton riots almost two decades before (Scarman, 1981), is a watershed in the history of policing the United Kingdom. It comes at a time when the work of the police has increasingly come under concerted public and political scrutiny. As the 'politics of law and order' gradually became entrenched within the Conservative Party of Mrs Thatcher, the police were originally conceived as the 'thin blue line' that separated the community from a variety of threats and dangers, and allowed us all to sleep safely in our beds. Thus they were to be congratulated, rewarded and given greater resources, at a time when others in the public sector were facing privatisation and market testing. Indeed, at the 1985 Conservative Party Annual Conference, Mrs Thatcher maintained that 'if they [the police] need more men, more equipment, they shall have them' (quoted in Rawlings, 1991). Only as the 1980s wore on were questions beginning to be asked about how 'effective' the British police were at controlling crime, or, in effect, at giving a return for the money that had been invested in them. The crime rate continued to go up, clear-up rates continued to fall and a series of miscarriage cases, often involving Irish suspects, began to undermine public confidence that the police were in fact as impartial as they were being portrayed in TV dramas and documentaries. Others also began to question the use of the police by the Government during the miners' strike and at a variety of other picket lines, which further served to undermine their status as servants of an increasingly diverse and multicultural community.

Neither did the police help themselves by adopting tactics that might have enhanced their standing within the community. The iconic PC — later Sergeant — George Dixon, who patrolled his beat and got to know people within the community, would have found little in common either with the 'panda' system, which served to distance the police from the community, or with the increasing amount of 'kit' that was made available to the police. Flame retardant jump suits; new helmets with visors that disguised and de-personalised, CS gas and extendable batons seemed to belong more to the world of *Robocop* than to the streets of Birmingham, Cardiff, Glasgow or London. Yet, as anyone who knows anything about policing will tell you, 'patrolling the beat' is extraordinarily ineffective for catching criminals and stopping crime. For example, one study by the Home Office estimated that a patrolling police officer was likely to pass within 100 yards of a crime in progress once every eight years (Clarke and Hough, 1984). So this growing 'professionalism' of the police and the tactics that they adopted were in part an attempt to do something about the rising crime rate, and indeed the changing nature of crime itself. Criminals have rarely accepted arrest as 'a fair cop, guv', but during the 1980s the police had to respond to an increased incidence of armed robbery and indeed mainland terrorism by the IRA.

This tension between the idea of serving the community, while at the same time being faced with increasing demands to be effective at controlling crime, has continued into the new century. It pulls our police in two different directions. On the one hand it demands the police to be sensitive to the needs of the various groups and sub-groups who make up our communities. From ethnic minorities, to the rights of gay people; from the needs of the victims of rape and domestic violence, to the concerns of those who do not wish new roads to be opened or animals transported abroad. This in turn leads to pressure on the police to recruit people from diverse backgrounds, rather than only those who are white, male and working class. On the other hand there are demands on the police to detect and prevent crime, which might be best done by employing technology, such as CCTV, or using covert surveillance and paid informants — with all the implications that this has for individual rights.

As the 1980s gave way to the 1990s these pressures seemed to become even greater. First, appalling crimes, such as the murder of the toddler James Bulger in 1993, and the ever-present reality of drugs in our communities kept crime high on the political agenda and policing at the forefront of the Government's response. These concerns also served to create a consensus between the two main political parties, so that by 1997 Jack Straw, at the time the Shadow Home Secretary, was able to offer cross-party support for Michael Howard's Crime (Sentences) Bill, which has subsequently become law. Mr Straw has since become Home Secretary, and his own Crime and Disorder Act has increased the pressure on the police to intervene in society through 'anti-social behaviour orders' and night curfews. Seemingly responding to what has been characterised as a 'Dutch auction' of 'toughness' on crime (Wilson and Ashton, 1998), policing tactics such as 'zero tolerance' were imported from New York and transported on to the streets of Cleveland and Middlesborough by Superintendent Ray Mallon. This intrusive style of policing, which in the short term appears to produce very dramatic results, has found favour with Mr Straw, who in power has urged people to 'have a go' if they witness a crime being committed and who while in opposition was scathing about aggressive beggars and 'squeegee merchants'. However, Superintendent Mallon is currently suspended from duty, although the largely white and homogenous citizens of Middlesborough have been overwhelming in their support of their erstwhile police chief.

Secondly, closer scrutiny of the police by the Audit Commission, an independent and powerful body set up to examine 'the three 'Es' — economy, effectiveness and efficiency — within the public sector, began to have an impact on how to judge policing performance. Indeed, the Audit Commission went further than simply measuring performance, and in encouraging the police to become more proactive and less reactive, it developed a model of policing which is optimistic in relation to what we can expect of our police as service deliverers of crime control. In short, it developed a model which is orientated towards controlling crime through prevention and detection, and thus improving clear-up rates. All this, according to the Commission, would lead to 'the ultimate prize for the police [which] is the development of a strategy in which the crime rate could be brought under control' (quoted in Morgan and Newburn, 1997). While we do not believe that this is possible, and will argue so below, there is no doubt that the Audit Commission has had a major impact on successive Governments' thinking about the role of the police in society. We detect its influence on the 1993 White Paper on *Police Reform*, which simply stated that the 'main job of the police is to catch criminals' (Home Office, 1993, at para. 2.2), and on the inquiry into the rank structure, pay and conditions of service of the police, conducted by Sir Patrick Sheehy, the Chairman of British American Tobacco. Indeed, the Sheehy Inquiry was published just days after the White Paper, and amongst a stream of recommendations, many of which caused uproar within the police, it stated that its intention was to 'reward good performance and penalise bad' (Sheehy, 1993).

Nonetheless, the police have at least attempted to respond more positively to the competing tensions of serving the community and controlling crime. For example, ethnic minority recruitment is high on every police force's agenda and there are now openly gay and lesbian police officers, who even have their own web site. The National Criminal Intelligence Service (NCIS) and the National Crime Squad (NCS) were established under the terms of the Police Act 1997 to fight crime on a more national scale, and a former Chief Constable, Keith Hellawell, has become a 'Drug Tsar' to coordinate Government policies controlling the spread of drugs into our society. There are more armed officers routinely patrolling than ever before, although unique amongst Western democracies, British police officers are usually unarmed in their day-to-day dealings with the public, even if CS canisters and side batons rather detract from this non-threatening and service orientated image.

But down which road are our police expected to travel — are they servants of the community, or 'crime busters'? If the former, how are they to respond to the realities of racism that the Macpherson Report has demonstrated, and how are they to regain the trust that has been lost in them by the Afro-Caribbean community? If the latter, how are we to protect our civil liberties from the intrusions of the police in the name of 'fighting crime'? Is it possible to do both at the same time? How will our politicians respond to worsening crime figures and the growing internationalisation of crime and criminals? And what of the police themselves? Can they continue to employ tactics that are costly but ineffective, and will they be able to respond to the challenges of policing a multi-cultural, pluralistic community, with its own agenda of what it is to be British in the new Millennium? And to what extent will the police themselves reflect that agenda?

This book is concerned with answering these questions. It will develop some of the themes to which this Introduction has drawn attention, especially in relation to racism, the media portrayal of the police, and how to respond to the demands for greater police efficiency, effectiveness and professionalisation. It will also raise other issues to which the police will have to respond, such as privatisation, civilianisation and voluntarisation, and the increasing desire of some citizens to purchase their own forms of policing. We will attempt to provide a context within which these questions can be answered, but throughout we are mindful that there are limits to what it is that the police can be expected to achieve. After all, crime does not exist in a vacuum but responds to the changing realities of our culture and society. It is no accident, for example, that the sustained growth in the crime rate that we have alluded to has occurred at the same time that income inequality — the gap between rich and poor in society — has increased (Harker, 1996). None of the agencies of the criminal justice system can be expected to 'control' crime, or indeed even detect it, and asking the police to do so is akin to asking Canute to hold back the sea.

SO, WHAT SHOULD EVERYONE IN BRITAIN KNOW ABOUT THE POLICE?

It is our argument that the police currently have a very limited impact on crime, spend little time on crime prevention and are just as limited in the role that they play in relation to crime detection. Yet, given that their work has become increasingly defined by these criteria, we are destined to spend more and more money on the police, in the hope that they will ultimately fulfil these tasks and responsibilities. It is our contention that we need to re-evaluate the contribution that the police can actually make to rendering our country safer, and base our judgement of them on that re-evaluation. It does not help if politicians, the media or indeed representatives of the police themselves continue to claim that 'more Bobbies on the Beat', 'less paperwork' or 'access to weapons' will contribute to a safer Britain when all the available evidence points in another direction. Ultimately the public needs to determine what it wants of the police, and to make that decision it needs access to the relevant information. At present such access is absent, but we hope that this book serves as a starting point.

All of what we have described needs to be placed in the context of the history of policing, the nature of the relationships that the police have with Police Authorities and the Home Secretary, and of course the reality of crime in the UK. The nature of the organisation of the policing system which we have today is the product of decisions taken in the early 19th century, and Chapter 1 provides a largely critical historical account of the police. As such it traces the development of the police from the establishment of the New Police in 1829 to the Royal Commission on the Police 130 years later, and the subsequent Police Act of 1964. At the conclusion of this historical introduction we discuss developments in the 1970s and 1980s, such as the Brixton riots and the miners' strike, which created new pressures on the police, as well as alluding to greater scrutiny of their work in relation to clearing up crime.

Chapter 2 continues building a context for our later discussions by describing the nature of policing and de-bunking some of the fallacies that exist about what the police do and have done. We also build on our short historical introduction, and highlight some of the key developments of policing in the 1980s and 1990s. Chapter 3 describes what is currently known about police performance, by looking at clear-up rates against the background of a rising crime rate. In describing the police's impact on crime we begin to challenge the optimistic impression given by the Audit Commission that the police can be an effective 'crime control' agency, for it is our belief that the answers to the crime problem do not lie within policing — a theme that we return to in later chapters.

Chapter 4 considers police governance. By this we mean to whom the police are accountable. We discuss the Police Complaints Authority (PCA) and Her Majesty's Inspectorate of Constabulary, as well as considering the role of the Home Secretary, chief constables and the Association of Chief Police Officers. Building on this, Chapter 5 looks at the issue of corruption. We discuss malpractice within the police, 'noble cause corruption', and the spate of miscarriage cases which have bedevilled the criminal justice system. We also describe the continuing difficulties experienced by those members of the public who wish to bring a complaint against the police, and the difficulty that police forces themselves seem to face when they attempt to root out and prosecute corrupt officers.

Many will regard Chapter 6 as revealing one of the greatest challenges currently to be faced by the police — how to police black or Asian communities. We describe and present statistics that reveal a pattern of racism against ethnic minorities, and look in depth at the impact of the Stephen Lawrence case on the future of policing. In doing so we also echo an earlier theme, i.e., the difficulty that black officers have within police culture, and the corresponding difficulties that are experienced when trying to recruit staff from ethnic minorities. We also describe the impact of policing on Muslim communities.

Chapter 7 considers 'police culture'. Who becomes a police officer, and why? Building on a reflexive diary kept by one of our former students who has become a police officer, and on interviews with serving and retired officers, we present a picture, a 'snap-shot' of the 'career culture'. In doing so we examine the sexual and racial harassment of fellow police officers, and the gulf that often exists between what 'rank and file' officers and those who manage or represent those officers believe. Chapter 8 looks at others who have a responsibility for 'policing'. Based on original research undertaken in Doncaster, we discuss the growth of private security and the tension that this creates between the police and those who are concerned with crime prevention and detection in the hope of making a profit.

Chapter 9 is our own vision of how we would want policing to develop in this country — a vision of how we should police the

Millennium. This vision takes the issues, initiatives and interests that we have outlined, and weaves them into a picture of policing which is accountable and realistic, blending the best techniques from home and abroad. We hope that Commander Waiganjo would approve.

METHODOLOGY

This book has used a variety of research techniques and is based on both primary and secondary sources. In relation to the former, we have walked the streets of Doncaster with an ex-bouncer and reformed convict who is selling security door-to-door to the people of Balby; ridden in police cars; participated in police operations in Derby and Devon and Cornwall; travelled to Europe to look at policing abroad; and drunk too many cups of tea in a variety of police canteens. Open-ended interviews with police officers of different grades, sexes and sexual orientation have been conducted, transcribed and theorised into an account of 'policing' from the front-line, and an ex-student kept for us a reflexive diary of his journey from university to police academy and how he 'became' a police officer.

Secondary sources are cited throughout the book. Of note, we return time and again to our historical perspectives, and are conscious of the fact that the police we have today are a product of decisions, tensions and policies adopted in the past. Academics interested in the police might be disappointed that a more consciously theoretical approach has been avoided, but — in keeping with our previous work in this genre — we are keen that the debate about who our police are, and how we are policed as a society, should have the broadest possible readership. So while this the book will be of interest and use to undergraduates studying criminology, criminal justice and public policy, we are just as concerned to attract the general reader — the so-called 'man and woman in the street' — for it is they who experience policing and who are too often denied access to information, analysis and criticism related to this important agency of the criminal justice system. We have also ensured that the book is accessible in terms of length. Despite the challenging nature of our conclusions, we have deliberately focused these within 204 pages. Those who wish to pursue how these conclusions have been researched should be guided by the references we have provided throughout the text.

Lastly, it should be noted that one of the authors is a former Chief Superintendent of Police with over 30 years' experience. His insight has been invaluable, bridging the gap between 'ivory tower' and the patrolling beat constable. Another of the authors is a campaigning journalist who has made his reputation in exposing miscarriages of justice, often caused by malpractice within the police. The third author is someone who has worked as a Prison Governor, and in this capacity his work brought him into daily contact with the police. In that sense the book has also been a truly collaborative effort, challenging each of the authors to put aside prejudice and assumption in an effort to formulate a synthesis of who the police are and how they might be developed. The result — we hope — is not a series of compromises and pulled-punches, but a genuine and passionate account of what everyone in Britain should know about the police.

1 A Short History of Policing

INTRODUCTION

This short historical chapter is divided into two distinct halves. In the first we outline some of the major influences on the origins and development of the police forces of England and Wales. In doing so we have adopted Emsley's 'common sense' definition of what is meant by 'the police': 'The bureaucratic and hierarchical bodies employed by the state to maintain order and to prevent and detect crime' (Emsley, 1991, at 1).

This definition is not without difficulties. Many other organisations and individuals are just as involved with maintaining order and preventing crime, such as gamekeepers or security staff, and recently — a theme taken up in later chapters — there have been several pilot initiatives which have seen local residents paying for private firms to patrol their streets, a function previously viewed as being the preserve of 'the police'. Similarly, the use of the words 'employed by the state', as Emsley himself acknowledges, suggests that there is a 'national police force' (something which was feared and resisted from the very beginnings of the New Police) despite the operational differences of the 43 police forces of England and Wales, and despite separate policing arrangements in Scotland and Northern Ireland. However, this definition does allow us a way to differentiate between those police officers paid for by central or local government, and those staff of private security firms who have become increasingly important in fulfilling what were once seen as police duties (Morgan and Newburn, 1997, at 44–73).

Throughout this chapter we remain conscious of earlier historiographical debates in police histories which can be characterised as 'Whig' and 'revisionist'. In short, 'Whig' histories see the origins and development of the police from 1829 onwards as progressive and rational, based on a desire to improve on the old parochial systems which could no longer cope with sustained increases in crime and disorder. These Whig histories — especially the works of Charles Reith (1938, 1943, 1948) — view the New Police as essentially the answer to the problem of crime, and as such are less interested with how 'crime' itself came to be defined, by whom, and to what ends. Thus they presuppose a consensus in society, despite the obvious inequalities in Victorian England in relation to class, wealth, race, sex and power.

Revisionist interpretations of the origins and development of the New Police probably start with Robert Storch (1975), who, unlike those writing within the Whig tradition, began to see the police as an instrument to be used by those with power to discipline the growing urban, working class. And while this crude oversimplification does not do justice to the far more sophisticated arguments of the revisionists, it ably demonstrates that the idea of 'consensus' in society — taken for granted in Whig interpretations — was instead something which was contested. Indeed, it is no small matter that the early years of the New Police were to see sustained attempts to establish a new level of decorum and order in the streets, where many working class people spent their leisure time, but who attracted criticism in relation to their gambling, drinking, prostitution and general disorderliness.

Theoretically this book is informed by the best of both of these traditions, but also by much more besides. It springs from the personal experiences of one of the authors, having worked as a chief superintendent of Police, including time spent with the Inspectorate of Police, and from the campaigning tradition of someone who works in journalism and is a specialist in miscarriages of justice. Yet it is also infused with primary and secondary academic research. Most notably, in relation to the former, we undertook primary research into the development of different private security firms offering patrolling services in Doncaster and Birmingham. Similarly, original research was undertaken in the United States in relation to zero tolerance policing. Thus, while the book happens to offer a critical analysis of the police, and is clearly sympathetic to the revisionist tradition, it remains rooted in the practical concerns of policing, and how these concerns affect the public.

Inevitably, as with any short history, we can deal only with historical 'highlights', although clearly the remainder of the book will expand upon the issues that this chapter raises. Thus those familiar with police history will recognise in the first half of the chapter the dates 1829 and 1856; and in the latter half, 1930 and 1964. For those less familiar with police history, these dates relate to the establishment of the Metropolitan Police by Sir Robert Peel in 1829; the County and Borough Police Act 1856; the celebrated case of *Fisher v Oldham Corporation* in 1930; and the Police Act 1964, which established more clearly the power of the Home Secretary, as opposed to the police committee, over the work of the Chief Constable. However, to infuse this short history with some colour, we will use as a source document to illustrate several of the themes which will emerge Sir Robert Mark's idiosyncratic autobiography — *In The Office of the Constable* (Mark, 1978).

Sir Robert Mark, a former Commissioner of the Metropolitan Police and chief constable of Leicester, is obviously not an impartial source. However, his autobiography is of note for several reasons. First, as befits any historical introduction, he neatly straddles the periods under discussion. Having been recruited in 1937, he was clearly aware of — and vividly describes — policing in an earlier generation. Indeed he was trained by policemen of the Victorian period. Thus he provides a glimpse of the 'canteen culture' of the police in the first half of the century. Similarly, as befits someone of his rank writing an autobiography, he offers some striking assessments of what will happen to the police in 'the future', after his retirement in 1977. Secondly, we have used Mark's autobiography as he himself was a Commissioner at the forefront of issues which have remained important for the police today. Most obviously, Mark had to deal with the Notting Hill riots in 1976, and consequently with the policing of ethnic minority communities in London; he had to combat increased terrorist activity in the city, most obviously by Provisional Irish Republican Army; and he spearheaded efforts to tackle police corruption. Lastly, Mark was perhaps the first senior policeman who genuinely recognised the need to use the media to shape and inform an understanding of police practice. He appeared, for example, on *Desert Island Discs*, and gave the Dimbleby Memorial Lecture in 1973; but more than this, it was he who was responsible for changing the force's policy of dealing with the media, from 'tell them only what you must' to 'withhold only what you must'. In so doing Mark carved for himself a place in police history as being in the vanguard of those who wanted to manage news in relation to how the police were reported, a development that he himself describes as 'one of the most important changes in my time at the Yard' (Mark, 1978, at 134, 135). For our purposes, what is important is that he left a record of his time as a policeman, as he saw it, which is comparatively rare.

However, we are also conscious that the Metropolitan Police are not 'the police'. In an effort to add some regional flavour to the chapter, we also use examples from outside London to look at how the police were organised and how they carried out their work. In particular we look at the development of the New Police in Birmingham, which was a reluctant convert to their cause. We argue that Birmingham's relation to the New Police mirrors their gradual acceptance throughout the country, based on the working philosophy of the 'prevention of crime'.

BEGINNINGS

In September 1829, the first constables of the Metropolitan Police began patrolling the streets of London, under the command of Colonel Charles Rowan and Richard Mayne, based at Scotland Yard. Wearing blue uniforms and top hats — to distinguish them from soldiers who wore scarlet tunics — and carrying only truncheons, traditional Whig historians like to see these 'New Police' as the inevitable consequence of Government — in the shape of Sir Robert Peel — responding to rising levels of crime. One historian, for example, has even gone as far as to characterise Georgian England as 'the golden age of gangsterdom' (Reith, 1938, at v), and indeed Peel himself does seem to have used some crude criminal statistics to help him push the new policing legislation through the House of Commons after several failed attempts (Emsley, 1991, at 25).

The same Whig historians would also like to characterise the New Police as more efficient than the night watchmen and 'thief takers' that they had replaced, but at the same time as the logical extension of other policing initiatives within the City, such as Henry Fielding's Bow Street Runners. Indeed Fielding, a novelist and Bow Street magistrate, his half-brother, Sir John Fielding, and Patrick Colquhoun do deserve to occupy a place in any history of our police, but far from being the logical extension of the Bow Street Runners, the Metropolitan Police operated in tandem with their earlier counterparts until 1839, when constables in the office of the stipendary magistrates could become members of the Metropolitan Police.

This last observation should remind us that in effect, between 1829 and 1839, there were at least two organised systems of policing within the capital. The oldest was based on the work of the 'trading' justices, such as Fielding at Bow Street, who were paid fees for performing judicial tasks. One such task was to pursue offenders, and Fielding and others employed gangs of professional thief takers to fulfil this obligation. Indeed householders would pay a local rate to employ watchmen to guard over their property — largely to combat fear about property crime — and by 1828 Fielding had a force which consisted of a Horse Patrol of 54 men and six officers; a Dismounted Patrol of 89 men and 12 officers; a Night Foot Patrol of 84 men and 18 officers; and a Day Foot Patrol of 24 men and three officers (Emsley, 1991, at 20). One advantage that these patrols had over the New Police was that they were accountable at a local level, whereas the latter were accountable to the Home Secretary — in truth the greatest difference between the Metropolitan Police and the thief takers.

It should also be noted that in these early days of the New Police there was a great deal of movement between the Metropolitan Police and constables in the offices of the stipendary magistrates. Emsley suggests that this was as a result of the fact that the latter could earn higher wages, given that they were paid on the basis of fees rather than a fixed wage as the New Police were. In effect this was an entrepreneurial system, and as such often open to abuse. Furthermore, many complained that they were paying significantly more for the New Police than they had been paying in the past, and many parishes petitioned the Government for control over the police and threatened to withhold money if this was not forthcoming (Emsley, 1991, at 27). They petitioned in vain.

Thus the development of the New Police was neither inevitable, nor necessarily a better alternative to those police whom they replaced, and their gradual acceptance had as much to do with continued, well-placed political support as with their ability to 'take thieves'. What characterised the New Police from their predecessors was that they were an instrument of Government, whereas the constables in the office of the magistrate represented a decentralised and locally accountable system of policing.

BIRMINGHAM AND THE NEW POLICE

Some insight into the organisation of the New Police in London can be gauged by comparing developments in Birmingham, especially after the Metropolitan Corporations Act of 1835 allowed the 'New Police' to spread outside of London. While the provincial forces which were set up by the Act were answerable to the local authority, Birmingham — along with Bolton and Manchester — had a centrally controlled police force between 1839 and 1842, as a result of emergency measures being taken by Parliament from fear of a Chartist uprising. Thus Birmingham between these years had a police force constituted along similar lines to the Metropolitan Police, and an investigation into its origins, culture and development can be used to reflect upon policing in general, and the New Police in particular.

Francis Burgess, an ex-Army officer, commanded Birmingham's New Police, and from the outset the city was hostile to him and his constables (Weaver, 1994, at 289). Yet by the time that control of the police returned from Parliament to the town council, this hostility had all but ebbed away. Thus, with only a little oversimplification, we can see in Birmingham's gradual acceptance of the New Police a trend that was to be replicated elsewhere. Their success seems to have been as a consequence of their ability both in the prevention and the detection of crime, reflecting Burgess's belief that crime fighting was a 'science' which was best applied through centralised, coordinated activity. Indeed, prior to 1839, policing in the city was de-centralised, and the Watch itself had only 160 men, not all of whom served the whole year round and who received little by way of supervision or training.

Burgess had some 293 men at his disposal — leading to criticisms that he was at the head of a 'standing Army' — but it was his use of these men that characterised the New Police in the city. Burgess divided Birmingham up into a series of beats, and each police constable was given a beat card that described the route that had to be walked. A sergeant was assigned to a series of beats, and a police inspector would make spot checks on the sergeants. The watchword for the constable was 'vigilance', and he was expected not only to get to know who lived on his beat, but also to check doors, locks, shutters and windows. The goal was to prevent crime from happening, and Burgess went as far as suggesting that if a burglary did occur on a constable's beat then that constable must have been at fault.

As with the Metropolitan Police, Burgess's constables did not carry weapons, and so walked their beat with a truncheon and a pair of handcuffs. Burgess also employed extra men during special occasions in the city, such as Chartist marches, and even went as far as employing 'plain clothes policemen'. Other preventative measures initiated by Burgess included ensuring that the street lights were switched on during the summer as well as the winter months and, as with his Metropolitan counterparts, developing a small team of detectives.

The success of Burgess's force has been measured by Michael Weaver (1994), who compared the number of people arrested and taken into custody in 1838–1839 with those taken into custody during the first full year of Burgess's New Police operating in Birmingham. In the earlier year the old police had taken 2,752 people into custody — a figure improved upon by Burgess's men by some 220 per cent, as they took 6,150 people into custody during their first year in operation. Nonetheless, even though Burgess could point to this success he still lost his job, and control of the force returned to the Town Council in 1842. It is significant, though, that no great changes were made to the style of policing that Burgess had introduced — a testament to winning Birmingham over to the New Police, even if they did dispense with Burgess's services.

POLICING THE VICTORIAN PERIOD: THE COUNTY AND BOROUGH POLICE ACT 1856

What had happened in Birmingham can be seen as indicative of what happened in the rest of the country. From the very uncertain beginnings of 1829, Victorians gradually accepted the 'New Police' as part of the 'British way of life'. By the turn of the century, for example, they were openly being described as 'the best police in the World' — a symbol of Britain, and increasingly part of her cultural identity. *The Times* (24 December), for example, concluded in 1906 that 'our police force is a credit to the men who are responsible for it, and a source of pride to every Englishman'. There are of course difficulties with this description, especially as it gives the impression that by this date there was a single, centralised national police force in the country. In fact there were three types of police at this time: the Metropolitan Police; the County Police, answerable to the standing joint committees; and the Borough Police, who were accountable to the local Watch Committee. It should also be remembered that even after the Local Government Act 1888, there were still some 183 separate police forces, and as late as 1945 there were 131 forces.

Neither should we accept that *The Times* spoke for all Victorians. Far from being 'domestic missionaries' (Storch, 1975), bringing a sense of decorum to working class areas, many poorer Victorians resented the New Police bitterly, given that their lives were becoming increasingly regulated and controlled. Indeed, one historian has gone so far as to suggest that policing during this period merely reflected 'an increasingly prim middle class view of propriety in public places' (Lustgarten, 1986, at 40). Again demonstrating the conflict between policing and the populace Emsley, (1991, at 231) quotes evidence presented to the 1908 Royal Commission on the Duties of the Metropolitan Police which suggests that between 1903–1906 on average 2,500 men were injured as a result of assaults made on them while performing their duties. Although these figures have to be used with care, they do at least suggest that the streets were still an area which was contested, and that one group's idea of decorum was another's idea of interference and control. Similarly, music hall jokes and songs about the police were commonplace, reflecting something of how people regarded their presence. The most famous is still largely misunderstood, given that it has been re-interpreted in our own era to reflect the reliability of the police, but as it was sung originally the idea that 'if you want to know the time — ask a policeman' was meant to suggest that police 'acquired' watches from drunks on their way home as they patrolled their beats.

Nevertheless, the Victorian period saw the police cement a place within British culture, and become a feature of contemporary comment and political initiative. Yet a variety of questions should still interest us. Who became a police constable, and what sort of 'canteen culture' (to use a more modern phrase) existed? What did a police constable actually do, and how was he held accountable for his actions? And, a question of no less interest today, were the police actually effective?

Peel had been very clear that recruits to the New Police should neither be 'gentlemen', nor have a military background — although this latter stipulation became increasingly difficult to sustain. Instead, new recruits were to be 'respectable' young working class men, under the age of 35, fit, literate and, according to Emsley (1991, at 191), 'blessed with a perfect command of temper'. The traditional view has been that most recruits were agricultural labourers, although this has been disputed. Sir Robert Mark, writing about his decision to join the police in the 1930s, for example, probably captures something of the realities of those who joined, and why:

> Jobs were valuable in 1937 and unemployment . . . meant what it said. It was really one of H.G. Wells's short stories that put into my head the idea of joining the police. It contained the sentence 'In the country of the blind the one-eyed man is King'. My reasoning ran thus. You have thrown away any chance of an academic career, or a job in public service needing academic qualifications, but you are fit, good at games and not entirely stupid. Why not take a job without popular appeal in which those qualifications will give you a positive advantage? With that in mind I applied to join the Manchester police . . . My father protested that it was only one step better than going to prison. (Mark, 1978, at 16–17)

We can also be certain about one aspect of recruitment — recruits were male, and even as late as 1939 there were only 246 female constables. New, unmarried recruits had to ask permission to wed, and while married men were preferred as constables — in the belief that this would make them less likely to associate with any prostitutes that they might encounter — a woman married to a police constable was not expected to work and had to be of 'good character'. All of this clearly reflected and re-enforced a largely working class culture that was rough and masculine. New recruits lived in 'barracks' — implying a sense of military discipline and rather undermining the original intention of not recruiting from the Army — and had to appear smart at all times, with their faces shaved and hair neatly cut. Some insight into the difficulties associated with conforming with this culture can be gained from information provided to a Parliamentary Committee of 1834, that of the 2,800 constables serving in 1830, only 562 remained four years later. And four out of every five who had been dismissed from the service had been so as a result of drunkenness. Indeed the particular association between the police and drink was again well captured by the Victorian music hall:

If you want to get a drink, ask a p'liceman!
He will manage it, I think, will a p'liceman!
If the pubs are shut or not
He'll produce a flowing pot
He can open all the lot, can a p'liceman!

Robert Mark was still able to remember that even as the late as the 1930s, 'many pubs and breweries in my early days in the police used to leave bottles of beer outside at night for the patrolling policeman' (Mark, 1978, at 18).

From the outset the New Police were interested in crime prevention — a principle which we have already discussed more fully in relation to Burgess's initiatives in Birmingham (see pp. 15–16 above). The main method of achieving this goal was through patrolling the streets, with the majority of officers patrolling at night. Thus even the Victorian constable could complain that, far from being 'glamorous', the work of a police constable was routine and humdrum, and, with the introduction of police boxes, subject to scrutiny and supervision (given that these meant that constables were required to ring their stations from the boxes at fixed times). However, detective, as well as preventative, work was also undertaken, and by 1842 Mayne had convinced Sir James Graham — at the time Home Secretary — that two inspectors and six sergeants should be appointed. It is of course difficult to determine how successful the New Police were in their preventative and detective roles, although it is probably fair to argue that they did cope with street crime, although this was by no means universal. After all, the Jack the Ripper murders in 1886, and the moral panics associated with the end of transportation to Australia which resulted in large numbers of convicts being released back on to London's streets, suggest that the New Police were no panacea to crime or criminals.

The County and Borough Police Act 1856 was the first significant centralising force within policing but, as with the legislation that had introduced the New Police in 1829, its passage was not without incident. That the Act was passed at all can be explained by two factors. First, it was supported from the outset by Lord Palmerston, originally while he was Home Secretary in the early 1850s, and thereafter as Prime Minister from 1855. Thus, like the legislation passed in 1829, the 1856 Act benefited from significant political support, and had been rooted in a Parliamentary Select Committee which had been set up in April 1853 to look at 'adopting a more uniform system of police' (Emsley, 1991, at 50). Secondly, it is likely that a variety of social factors had led to increasing anxiety about crime. There are contemporary complaints, for example, about vagrancy, especially in the countryside, and the slow-down and eventual abolition of transportation meant that increasing numbers of those who had been convicted by the courts were ultimately being released back into the community. At the same time the outbreak of the Crimean War meant that the Army was abroad, and therefore any unrest — real or imagined — would have to be dealt with by domestic policing forces.

In essence the 1856 Act obliged local, or borough or county government to form police forces, thus seemingly maintaining a high degree of local control over the police, although this was gradually to be undermined by the growing power both of central Government and of chief constables. For example, in relation to the former, the Act introduced three new Inspectors of Constabulary, who were responsible to the Home Office and who were to issue certificates of efficiency to local forces. Such a certificate was a passport to government grants of a quarter of expenses related to clothing and pay, and was issued on the basis of the force's ability to perform drill, the number of constables in the force in relation to the size of the population, and the number of more senior officers who were able to perform supervisory roles. In 1874 this Treasury grant increased to one half of the cost of pay and uniform, and after 1914 to half of the total cost of the force. Thus the certificate of efficiency was a tool which could be used to effect greater centralisation and standardisation. The Inspectors also produced Annual Reports about their inspections, which in turn began to establish a culture of what policing was, or should be, about.

Part of that culture — and a theme which emerges directly from this short history — relates to the question of police 'independence', a doctrine which becomes enshrined in the Police Act 1964 but which in the earlier period revolves around the issue of whether there is a 'master-servant' relationship between a police constable and the Watch Committees which had been set up in 1835. Initially these committees took an active interest in how the police were organised in their locality; and more importantly they also had the power to dismiss a constable, including the head constable. Lustgarten (1986, at 37) reminds us that these powers were regularly exercised, and cites an example from Birmingham in 1880 when the head constable was opposed to a resolution of the Watch Committee and appealed to the Home Secretary. The Home Secretary refused to intervene and the head constable complied with the wishes of the Watch Committee. A similar situation would develop in Liverpool in 1890, when a moral-reforming Watch Committee ordered Captain Nott-Bower, the head constable, to close down the city's brothels. He advised against this policy, believing that it would waste time and effort and in the long run do little to stamp out prostitution, but was still required to carry out the wishes of the Watch Committee against his advice.

Robert Mark, writing about policing in the 1950s, was still able to describe with some feeling the power that a Watch Committee could exercise:

> ... the Watch Committee of a borough with its own police force exercised the power to appoint and to promote. It was the disciplinary authority. It also determined the size of the force and controlled its expenditure. All of these powers were to some extent subject to influence by the Home Secretary, whose Inspectorate of Constabulary determined the fitness of a force to receive the Exchequer grant of one half of its annual expenditure. Nevertheless the Watch Committee was in those days a power to be reckoned with and though disagreement between them and force administrators was often bitter, there was no doubt that the senior policemen involved were all the better administrators for having to deal with them. (Mark, 1978, at 58)

In 1950, Mark had himself to deal with the Oxford Watch Committee when he sought an appointment in the city. His description of his interview probably reveals that the power a Watch Committee exercised had as much to do with class and 'fitting in', as it had to do with specialist knowledge of police work or sound administrative abilities. He describes his interview in the following way:

> We were interviewed in the morning, the Watch Committee entertaining us to lunch to see if any of us ate with our feet. In those days the Oxford Watch Committee was required by law to include a number of members of the University. I sat at lunch on my best behaviour with a don on my left and a non-University member on my right. Over the soup the don remarked encouragingly, 'And where will you send your boy to school when you come to Oxford?' Even more

encouragingly, over the dessert the councillor dug me in the ribs and said, 'Got a lovely 'ouse for sale. Six thousand quid.' I really thought my ship was in. (Mark, 1978, at 60–61)

In fact Mark's ship did not come in on this occasion, but by January 1957 he had become chief constable of Leicester. Again, his description of what he did in those early days of taking charge of the Leicester force reveals the lingering influence of the Watch Committee over decisions that had to be taken. Indeed, on taking charge his first task was to send 'for the last few years' Watch Committee minutes [which] are always a good way to find out about the current and past problems' (Mark, 1978, at 62). Mark had inherited a force consisting of only one division of just under 300 men, which, with the CID, traffic and female officers, made up a total complement of 440. Within nine months he had obtained the 'approval of the Watch Committee and the Home Office' to increase the number of superintendents, so as to create three divisions, a new traffic department and a force administration department. As Mark indicates, 'this meant many promotions and a considerable boost to morale' (Mark, 1978, at 63).

The big issue which Mark had to deal with in Leicester was the fact that traffic in the city 'was in chaos', but before he could introduce the changes which he wanted he had to ensure that all the key stakeholders in the city were on his side. As an object lesson on how to deal with the competing demands placed on a reforming chief constable, Mark's account of how he implemented change, although clearly not impartial, is worth repeating at some length, for it reveals all the various interest groups and sources of power, and how to accommodate their often competing agendas.

First, Mark withdrew police officers who had been placed on point duty in the town, so as to allow the local newspaper — the *Leicester Mercury* — a free run through the traffic at distribution times. He also declined to accept any more free copies of the newspaper, and gave strict instructions that all parking laws had to be enforced 'without regard to wealth, politics or status'. (All quotes in this paragraph are taken from Mark, 1978, at 64–68.) As might be expected, the local newspaper was particularly opposed to this development, given that it had benefited from the previous arrangement, and Mark advises that his new policy became known as 'the Three Years War' — 'the reaction was pure Clochemerle'. However, Mark's enforcement of the parking laws was only the beginning of the changes he had planned. Next he introduced parking meters, established a 'traffic warden corps' and introduced fixed parking penalties. Instructions to the traffic wardens were circulated to the press — in an effort to win back media support — and included the comment that their efficiency would not be judged on the number of tickets issued, 'but by the freedom of your patrol areas from vehicles parked in contravention of the law'. In other words, 'prevention not prosecution was the primary objective'. Copies of the scheme were then sent to the clerk of the magistrates, and thereafter to members of the bench, as well as to the town clerk, who was working behind the scenes to establish a Traffic Committee 'on which the chairmen and vice-chairmen of all interested committees, watch, transport, finance, general purposes and highways were represented'. All of this effort was successful, for Mark suggests that as a result 'I was firmly established with the goodwill of my force, my Watch Committee, the city council and not by any means least important, the Press'.

FISHER v *OLDHAM* AND THE POLICE ACT 1964

We have spent some time describing Mark's dealings with various Watch Committees in the 1940s and 1950s because they reveal one of the important themes in the police's history. Namely, to what extent are the police independent of local political — or indeed any other form of — control? *Fisher* v *Oldham Corporation* and provisions within the Police Act 1964 deal with this issue.

The case of *Fisher* v *Oldham Corporation* [1930] 2 KB 364 is well known, and features in most standard accounts of police history (*cf.* Lustgarten, 1986; and Emsley, 1991, from which all the quotes that follow are taken). In brief, in 1930 a man named Fisher was falsely identified as a felon who was wanted on a charge of obtaining £150 by false pretences from a trader in Oldham. He was arrested in London and taken on warrant to Oldham. There the police recognised that a mistake had been made and Mr Fisher was released. He began an action seeking damages for false imprisonment, and directed his claim against Oldham Corporation who employed the police constables. In a crucial — and largely mistaken — judgment, Mr Justice McCardie concluded that 'a police constable is not the servant of the borough. He is the servant of the state, a ministerial officer of the central power, though subject in some respects, to local supervision and local regulation'. This judgment has been the subject of much speculation, but in essence it ignores the powers over constables that were conferred on Watch Committees by the County and Borough Police Act 1856 (see pp. 21–22 above). Nonetheless, according to the decision in *Fisher* v *Oldham*, a police constable was independent of local political interference — he was not 'a servant of the borough', but rather a 'ministerial officer of the central power'. What Robert Mark reveals is that while this might have become true in theory, Watch Committees remained a force to be reckoned with in practice.

Even so, an astute chief constable could manipulate the situation to his advantage by garnering Home Office and Inspectorate approval to push through initiatives over the heads of a reluctant Watch Committee, or appealling to the Home Office for support against the Watch Committee. However, this had to be done with some care, for even winning this type of battle might prove to be a Phyrric victory, as the case of Captain Athelstan Popkess, the chief constable of Nottingham, demonstrates.

Until the events of the 'Popkess affair', the chief constable of Nottingham might have become known to history solely as someone interested in the use of mobile two-way radio units for the prevention and detection of crime (Critchley, 1978, at 271). However, he has now become inseparable from the debate surrounding questions related to local, public accountability of the police and their constitutional position in the state. Briefly, in 1959 Popkess believed that there was corruption in the city's government, and he approached the Director of Public Prosecutions (DPP) with his suspicions. Acting on the advice that he received, he called in the Metropolitan Police to conduct an investigation, but this proved to be inconclusive, and the DPP advised that no further action should be taken. Unfortunately for Popkess, the Watch Committee discovered that an investigation had taken place and asked Popkess for a copy of the report. Popkess refused to comply, stating that law enforcement was his business and not the responsibility of the Watch Committee. As a result of his actions, the Watch Committee (exercising 19th-century powers still available to them) suspended Popkess, who was in turn reinstated by the Home Secretary (although by the end of the year he had retired).

The Popkess affair, and one or two other high-profile incidents, created a climate that sought to clarify some constitutional questions related to the police, and as a result a Royal Commission, chaired by Sir Henry Willink, was set up in January 1960. Who was in ultimate control of the provincial police? And if the answer was ultimately 'the Home Secretary', did that not raise the spectre of a 'national police force' which had no local accountability? Most of the Royal Commission's recommendations were incorporated into the Police Act 1964, which in essence developed the existing, rather confused system by accepting as its starting point the decision of Mr Justice McCardie in *Fisher* v *Oldham*. Consequently, local police committees were deprived of the legal responsibility for policing an area, and the Watch Committee's powers of appointment, discipline and dismissal were handed over to the chief constables — the real winners in the 1964 Act. In short, the boroughs fell into line with the counties, in that the chief constable had now the power to appoint, promote and discipline. The local police authority could call for annual reports from its chief constable, and was responsible for his or her appointment, and dismissal.

The Police Act 1964 also gave powers to the Home Secretary, in that he could call for reports from chief constables and also had to approve their appointment or dismissal. Perhaps more importantly, the Home Secretary, in the guise of 'efficiency' — which is nowhere defined (*cf.* Jefferson and Grimshaw, 1984, at 19) — could also promote co-operation between forces, and was given the power to amalgamate forces. This power was used in 1966 when Roy Jenkins reduced the number of forces from 117 to 49, and subsequently the Local Government Act 1972 reduced the number of forces still further to its current 43.

CONCLUSION

This short historical chapter has not been intended to provide a definitive account of police history. Indeed, it largely ends with the Police Act 1964, although it has alluded to developments thereafter. Rather we have attempted to highlight themes that emerge from a history of the police — themes which later chapters will develop. Of note, the chapter has drawn attention to the contested nature of policing in our history and to the reality that the police were not universally welcomed, despite traditional Whig history on this matter. Secondly, we have described something of what police work was about. From the outset this concerned crime prevention, rather than detection. Thirdly, we have described how the police were made accountable, how they were managed, and provided a little of the debate about police independence. Lastly, we have also revealed something of police culture by looking at their recruitment policies.

But what was to happen after 1964? Given the use that we have hitherto made of Robert Mark's autobiography, he can perhaps be given something of a 'last word'. For Mark the 'two great problems for the next generation of policemen' were:

> Resistance to political encroachment on their operational freedom, and exposure to the brunt of social change. By comparison with these two, crime is never likely to be more than the conventional costly nuisance it is today and terrorism, as today, in reality a comparatively insignificant issue. Freedom and public order, in the widest sense, must be the priorities for the police of tomorrow — and I mean free from domestic, not foreign masters. (Mark, 1978, at 290)

The first of Mark's problems is of course a return to the theme of police independence which we have already discussed, although his autobiography is less forthcoming as to how the police were to be made accountable in the future. However, it is perhaps the second problem — the 'brunt of social change' — which sets up our remaining chapters more adequately. How the police not only respond to an increasingly multi-racial and ethnically diverse society, but also how they manage these social changes within their own ranks become major preoccupations in the years after 1964.

Mark also wrote in an era before the advent of 'Key Performance Indicators' (KPIs) and the application of managerial techniques to the agencies of the criminal justice system, which within the police in the 1980s became known as 'policing by objectives'. As such, he could be rather dismissive of crime as a 'conventional costly nuisance', as he did not experience to the same extent that chief constables do today the need to demonstrate success in reducing crime. The drive for 'efficiency, effectiveness and economy' — the three 'Es' — is thus largely absent from what Mark wrote, but we cannot imagine a chief constable writing his or her memoirs today without including chapters outlining their successes in these areas. He also wrote just prior to the election of a Conservative Government in 1979, the riots in Brixton, Birmingham and Manchester, and the policing of the miners' strike in the 1980s. These events had major implications for how the police were organised, controlled and made accountable, and were inextricably linked to the 'politics of law and order'. In short, and rather crudely, the Conservatives became firmly established as the party of 'law and order', and were seen as being the natural ally of the police (*cf.* Wilson and Ashton, 1998). In recent years this situation has changed quite dramatically, and one can date that change to the re-moralisation of the law and order debate that took place after the murder of James Bulger in 1993. This tragic event has produced a political consensus between the two main political parties about law and order, and thus a less obvious link between representative bodies of the police and any one political party.

In the final passage of his autobiography, Mark — as one might expect of a senior, retiring policeman — returns to the idea of the police being an unique part of British culture, and as such as something in which we could all take pride. We need not accept his conclusion, but as an aspiration we too hope that the police:

> ... demonstrate collectively the qualities which make Britain, with all its anxieties and problems, still one of the most agreeable countries in the World, and are readily seen, with all their faults and virtues, as being amongst the best exemplars of it. (Mark, 1978, at 311)

The chapters that follow critically test that aspiration.

2   The Nature of Policing

INTRODUCTION

On 4 January 2000, an article appeared in the *Guardian*, which informed its readers that during 1999 West Yorkshire Police had reported a number of abuses of the 999 emergency telephone system. The article gave three examples: in one a man reported that two squirrels were fighting on his lawn; in another an elderly woman phoned because her knitting had become tangled; while in the third a young couple had handcuffed themselves together and had lost the key. Although one could raise a smile at these examples, and even understand the logic in the case of the handcuffed couple, all three cases represent misuse of a system which is intended to provide a response to genuine emergencies. Unfortunately such abuse is not unusual. The same article goes on to note that in the same year Thames Valley Police received 999 calls to report paranormal activity, sightings of Elvis, and even requests for taxis. Other police forces routinely report similar abuse, and indeed the other emergency services — the Fire Brigade and the Ambulance Service — have similar stories to tell.

Reports of this nature inevitably give rise to a range of reactions, from mild amusement to anger and frustration, but they should also give us cause for thought. On the one hand they illustrate some of the difficulties that the police face in coping with escalating and sometimes unreasonable demands at a time when their resources are static or even diminishing. On the other hand, however, they may give us some insight into the place that the police occupy in the minds of the public. Unreasonable or not, these examples represent situations with which ordinary people do not know how to deal. In these circumstances they turn to the police for help, advice and guidance. If that is indeed the case then it illustrates some of the complexities involved in modern policing, and represents the extreme end of a continuum of demand with which the police service must attempt to deal in one way or another.

The last 40 years have in fact been a time of almost continuous re-organisation and refocusing of policing, and yet we are faced with a serious problem. The problem, stated simply, is that we lack any clear consensus of what the police role is in a liberal democratic society. So is there anything that can help us to come to a better understanding of what the police are for, or indeed what the police do?

The police in England and Wales have always undertaken a range of activities which do not involve law enforcement and have little or nothing to do with crime. In the early years, for example, it was the police who operated the Fire and Ambulance Services. Over the years numerous regulatory and supervisory roles devolved upon the police, often because of their availability around the clock, but also because they were relatively cheap to employ. In more recent times many of these roles have been professionalised, but others remained throughout the 20th century. These regulatory functions have little to do with crime or disorder in the normal sense of those words, but they have had the effect of placing the police squarely in the centre of everyday life in Britain and almost everybody has a view about the nature of policing. In fact, we would contend that our ideas about policing are based on a number of commonly held fallacies.

POLICING — THREE FALLACIES

The first fallacy is that of the Golden Age. It is of course true that nearly every human endeavor has its Golden Age — a time in the indeterminate past when everything was better. The difference with policing is that the Golden Age is actually located in a specific time frame — broadly the time between the end of the Second World War and the middle of the 1960s, but specifically the late 1950s and early 1960s. Although the notion of the Golden Age seems to be firmly fixed in the minds of some commentators, it is a problematic concept. It is true that policing was different in the last half of the 1950s from what it is today, but there is little evidence that it was better. In fact the Royal Commission on the Police (Critchley, 1978) which reported in 1962 was established in part at least because of concerns about a lack of effective police accountability and fears of corruption and malpractice. In any event, the Golden Age effectively died in 1968 with the introduction of the policing scheme known as Unit Beat Policing.

The second of the fallacies is that of policing by consent. We pride ourselves in this country that the police are local in character and are not subject to Government control. We perpetuate a myth that there is an unspoken yet firmly based understanding between the police and the public as to what is expected, and what the police will do to ensure that these expectations are fulfilled. Yet in truth the notion of consent is a dubious one which has occupied the minds of academics and police historians. For example, Reiner (1992a) discusses the notion of policing by consent, while Waddington (1999) examines the notion of consent in the context of the exercise of police powers to stop and search citizens.

In fact the notion of consent received a considerable setback in the early 1980s when, following the inner-city disturbances of 1980 and 1981, Lord Scarman reported that communication had broken down between the police and the community. Lord Scarman's recommendation that effective communication should be re-established was enshrined in s. 106 of the Police and Criminal Evidence Act 1984, when police authorities were required to establish Police Consultative Committees as a forum for regular meetings between the police and the public. In fact a wealth of research since 1984 has concluded that the committees were generally regarded as irrelevant or ineffective; they were dominated by unrepresentative special interest groups and the police used them to set out their policies rather than to consult (see Reiner (1992a) and Morgan and Newburn (1997)).

The third fallacy is the notion of community policing. The term was first coined by Alderson (1979), who suggested that the police could (and should) play a central role in formulating, supporting and enforcing behavioural norms in society. Alderson's views largely fell on stoney ground in the UK, but were taken up in the United States and ultimately re-introduced here in the early 1990s as an antidote to the belief that the police had lost contact with the public during the 1970s and the 1980s. In this case the notion of community policing had changed subtly from Alderson's original conception, and was now used to describe the efforts made by the police to make their services more accessible to communities or localities which were seen as having particular problems with crime or disorder.

The fallacies of policing by consent and community policing are, of course, very closely related and share the notion that policing in England and Wales is essentially local in character. In some sense it is — there are 43 police forces, all of which have a local police authority which is drawn from representatives of the area, local councillors, magistrates and the 'great and the good'. Yet, as we will explain, the history of policing has been one of creeping centralisation since mid-Victorian times, and the Home Office now has far more influence on policing policy than does any local representation. We will also suggest that events in Europe are likely to push this trend even further in the years to come.

There is, however, another way in which this local character of policing is expressed, and that is in relation to the recruitment of police officers. In this case the argument is that police forces recruit locally and that communities are therefore policed by people who know and understand the subtleties of character and behaviour in an area, and are able to respond sensitively yet firmly when things go wrong. In fact even this assertion does not bear close scrutiny, and it is only very recently in police history that forces have begun to express a preference to recruit mainly from within their own areas. The police in Birmingham in the 1960s, for example, were made up of significant numbers of officers from Scotland, Wales and (to a lesser extent) Ireland, as well as large numbers of men from elsewhere in England. Where men (and it was at this time generally men who joined) did join from the Birmingham area, they were invariably posted to work in a different part of the city from where they were recruited. The Birmingham example is representative of the picture in other large, urban police forces. Rural forces were slightly different, in that recruits were often much more likely to come from within the local area, but again they were usually required to work well away from the place where they were brought up, and most rural police forces had policies to move officers around at regular intervals so that they never developed strong local connections and loyalties.

Nonetheless, for most of the history of policing there was a sense in which it had local character, and that was in organisational terms. Prior to 1964 there were 117 police forces in England and Wales, many of which were very small and which maintained a local identity. Policing was largely undertaken on foot and police stations were established within population centres. However, in 1966 the Home Secretary began to use his powers granted in the Police Act 1964 to amalgamate police forces on grounds of efficiency. By 1974 the number of forces had shrunk to the present 43. At the same time the increased use of motor cars, personal radios and computers enabled the police to centralise their operations in the name of efficiency, and to close many of the outlying police stations and replace them with telephones. Police forces re-drew their internal boundaries to fit in with their own priorities, borders between police divisions were set to ensure that the workload for each area was roughly equal, and often identifiable communities found that an administrative boundary had arbitrarily been drawn through rather than round them. What had been local suddenly became unfamiliar and remote.

So, if so much of what we think of policing is based on fallacy, what do we in fact know? What research tells us is that we know a great deal about how the police are organised and what the police do (and what they do not do). An examination of the history of policing gives us an insight into the original intention of police reformers in the 19th century, and should lead us to question the commonly held assumption that policing is primarily about crime.

ORTHODOXY AND REVISIONISM

As we discussed in Chapter 1, there are two distinct ways of interpreting police history. The orthodox view sees the development of organised policing as a direct response to the growing crime problem in urban centres during the Industrial Revolution, while the revisionist view sees policing as an essentially repressive activity intended to control the working classes and ensure a compliant, disciplined workforce for the emerging capitalist economy. That debate will not be resolved here, but there does seem to be some evidence to suggest that it was public order rather than crime which was uppermost in the minds of the early police reformers. Waddington (1999), for example, argues that if crime had been of central importance, Peel and his colleagues would not have established the Metropolitan Police in the way that they did.

Similarly, if we examine the early histories of policing outside of London, it is difficult to escape the conclusion that disorder, or the fear of disorder, was uppermost in the minds of the police reformers. For example, the establishment of organised policing in Birmingham, Manchester and Bolton was a direct response by the Government to the threat to public order (and indeed the stability of the Crown) that was posed by Chartism. In Birmingham (see also Chapter 1) the situation was complicated by internal disputes about the establishment of the police force, and in July 1839 the city magistrates requested assistance from the Metropolitan Police to deal with an outbreak of serious rioting by Chartist sympathisers. A detachment of officers was sent to the city and sworn in as special constables. This was an unsatisfactory arrangement, and they managed to restore order only with the assistance of the Army. In August 1839, Parliament passed the Birmingham Police Act, which established a police force on exactly the same lines as the Metropolitan Police with a Commissioner reporting directly to the Home Secretary.

It thus seems perfectly clear that in some of our larger cities at least, it was disorder and not crime that was central to the drive to establish organised policing. It was really only after the threat posed by Chartism had died away that the Birmingham Police were re-organised on a model of local rather than central accountability similar to that which we would recognise today. Furthermore, Emsley (1991), in discussing the early years of the Metropolitan Police, cites various contemporaries of Peel disputing the assertion that the New Police could effectively combat crime. It should also be remembered that the Metropolitan Police had no Criminal Investigation Branch until the formation of the Detective Department in 1842.

Historians have also noted that the emergence of industrialised capitalism in the early part of the 19th century demanded a much more ordered workforce than had hither to been required. Not only was it necessary to control the unruly working classes who had during the 18th century resolved their grievances by the use of the riot, it was also necessary to regulate leisure activity to ensure a workforce that was sufficiently disciplined and physically fit to work for long hours in unpleasant and often unhealthy situations. Reiner (1998) believes that routine crime and disorderliness were seen as a threat to social organisation, and organised policing was perceived as the best and most efficient way of supplying the necessary levels of order. It was social order, therefore, that was considered to be more important than crime. As Emsley points out, 'What the new Police were especially good at

was apprehending those who had committed petty street offences ...
they were less successful in preventing burglary' (Emsley, 1991).

In many ways public disorder has remained at the forefront of
policing ever since. The last three decades of the 20th century could be
characterised as times of increasing unrest. Industrial disputes during
the 1970s led ultimately to the fall of two governments, those of Edward
Heath in 1974 and of James Callaghan in 1979. During the 1980s and
1990s we saw inner-city riots, the miners' strike of 1984/85 and
anti-poll tax riots in Trafalgar Square. Civil disobedience associated
with the anti-nuclear protests at Greenham Common, the Newbury
Bypass, the M3 extension and live animal exports, has placed increasing
demands on policing. In addition, the rise of so-called alternative
lifestyles, particularly associated with New Age travellers of the 1980s
and the early 1990s with their anarchic approach to life and attachment
to free music festivals, placed additional burdens on the police. Such
lifestyles were characterised in the media as a threat to civilised society,
which demanded increased police powers and for 'something to be
done'. More recently, the anti-capitalist, anarchist inspired demonstra-
tions in both the United States and in England have resulted in disorder
in our major cities, such as that which took place in Parliament Square
in London on May Day 2000 and 2001.

WHAT DO THE POLICE DO?

Patrolling the Beat

It is not just large-scale public disorder which causes us to question the
police role. Policing has been subject of academic study for 40 years
now, and during that time we have discovered a great deal about what the
police do. Here again, the notion that policing is primarily about crime is
challenged by the research data. Bayley (1996) describes research
undertaken between 1989 and 1993 in 28 police forces in five countries.
The picture that he presents is remarkably similar across countries and
jurisdictions. Patrolling is the single largest activity undertaken by the
police. Specialist criminal investigation and traffic make up most of the
remainder, these three together occupying 85 per cent of police time.

In England and Wales patrolling in uniform remains the most
common police activity, with about 55 per cent of a police force's

strength being classed as operational patrol. The purpose of uniform patrol was originally established in 1829 with the formation of the Metropolitan Police, when Richard Mayne, one of the two first Commissioners, informed the 'New Police' that their function was 'the prevention of crime, the protection of life and property and the preservation of public tranquillity' (quoted in Newburn, 1995). More recently the Association of Chief Police Officers (ACPO) defined police patrol as 'the overt presence whether on foot or mobile, of a locally accountable uniformed Police Constable who provides public reassurance and who is approachable and available to ensure an appropriate response from all resources of the Police Service to the needs and demands of the general public' (ACPO, 1995). Similarly, the Audit Commission, in its influential report *Streetwise* (1996a), stated that patrol is

far more than a uniform Constable walking the streets. It is the principal but not the only means by which the Police:

- respond appropriately to crime, other incidents and emergencies,
- maintain public order and tackle anti-social behaviour
- re-assure the public through a visible Police presence
- forge links with local communities to reduce problems of crime and nuisance
- gather intelligence especially in relation to crime and criminals.

What is interesting about these three quotations is that the ACPO definition excludes any direct reference to crime, whereas Mayne's original instructions and the Audit Commission's 1996 definition quite clearly place crime as central to the police function. It is true of course that crime can, and should, be included in the phrase 'needs and demands of the general public', but we are entitled to ask why it is that crime does not figure as central to the ACPO definition. The answer may be quite simple: the police have known for a very long time that patrolling is an extremely ineffective method of fighting crime.

Perhaps one of the best known investigations of police patrol is the *Kansas City Preventive Patrol Experiment* (Kelling *et al.*, 1974). This was an investigation carried out in the 1970s, where the amount of motor patrol activity was varied on different beats in the city. The study found that increasing or decreasing the levels of patrol had no significant effect on a range of measures. The measures included crime levels, fear of crime and public satisfaction with the police. But perhaps this is not too surprising. Most of the critics of policing in England and Wales during the 1970s and 1980s attributed the declining levels of public satisfaction and increasing crime rates experienced during this time to police officers abandoning foot patrol in favour of the motor car. So is foot patrol more effective? There is a less well-known study, undertaken in Newark, New Jersey (Police Foundation, 1981), where the level of foot patrols was manipulated in much the same way as in Kansas City. The effect on the crime rate was the same as in Kansas. In other words, there was no change, but there was an increased level of public satisfaction with the police and a decreased fear of crime.

Further evidence of the ineffectiveness of patrolling comes from a Home Office study undertaken in 1983 (Clarke and Hough, 1984), which estimated that a patrolling police officer in London was likely to pass within 100 yards of a burglary in progress once every eight years. The study goes on to acknowledge that the officer would not necessarily realise that the crime was taking place, or have much chance of catching the offenders. Notwithstanding all of the evidence, though, the fact is that the public like to see uniformed officers on the streets; they feel more secure and they feel that the police are available and 'doing something'. But what exactly are they doing?

The earliest academic research dates from 1964 and the publication of two significant pieces of work. Banton (1964), in a comparative study of police officers in Scotland and the United States, concluded that the officer on patrol acted primarily as a 'peace Officer rather than a law Officer'. Banton observed that most officers' time on the beat was spent in responding to requests for assistance from members of the public; often the incidents were never officially recorded, and when not responding the officers were engaged in what he described as 'supervising the beat'. At the same time, Cumming and his colleagues analysed telephone calls to the police in an American force and found that most related to personal problems or interpersonal disputes (Cumming, Cumming and Edell, 1964). Other studies have confirmed these early pieces of work. Reiss (1971) found that 80 per cent of calls from the public related to non-crime incidents while in 1973, Punch and Naylor, in a study of rural and urban policing in Essex, found that the proportion of crime-related incidents differed according to location, but service calls invariably outnumbered those concerned with crime (Punch and

Naylor, 1974). The Audit Commission has reported that around 60 per cent of calls to the police relate to incidents which are not crime based (Audit Commission, 1993). As Reiner (1992a) observes, this research evidence gave rise in the 1970s and 1980s to the notion that the police were performing a service rather than a law enforcement role. It is significant to note, however, that he goes on to acknowledge that this view was never held with any conviction by rank and file officers, who traditionally see crime fighting as their main role.

In reviewing all of this evidence we need to exercise some caution. A number of authors have pointed out that some incidents might have resulted in crime had they not been dealt with effectively at an earlier stage. Many relatively minor disputes have the potential to escalate into assault or criminal damage if not resolved by effective intervention. On the other hand, the definitions of what is a crime and what is appropriate intervention change over time. One of the best examples of this is domestic violence, which for many years was regarded as a non-criminal dispute but which is now treated very seriously by both the police and the criminal justice system as a whole. Nevertheless, the balance of police work until very recently was still weighted towards a more service-orientated approach, and Reiner's 1992 description of policing as 'order maintenance' still remains valid today.

Order maintenance — 'broken windows' and zero tolerance

It can, of course, be argued that crime and social order are inextricably linked and that any debate which seeks to separate them is mistaken. This is exactly the point made in the theory known as 'broken windows', developed in the 1980s by Wilson and Kelling in the United States. They argue that neighbourhoods descend into a spiral of crime and social disintegration when small acts of incivility and lawlessness go unremarked and unrectified. Incidents of graffiti, litter, criminal damage and rowdy behaviour are allowed to escalate because of official inertia and public apathy, and eventually crime, drug abuse and social disorganisation become the defining characteristics of the area (Reiner, 1992a). It is of course 'broken windows' which informed the so-called 'zero tolerance' policing strategy which is claimed successfully to have cleaned up the streets of New York. Similar strategies have also reported success in reducing crime in Hartlepool and Middlesborough in England, and in various cities in the United States. The term 'zero tolerance' was in fact rarely used in New York, but in Britain it found considerable support amongst politicians and the mass media prior to the 1997 General Election, and remains a popular media topic today.

The principle upon which zero tolerance is based is relatively simple. It aims to deploy police resources across a wide range of situations and activities to deal with low-level disorder, minor offences and serious crime. In practice, however, it seems to have led to a concentration of police efforts on behaviour which may be regarded as anti-social, and which on occasion is criminal, but which has its roots much more in social and economic disadvantage. Zero tolerance may remove problems from the street, but it does not deal with the underlying causes. While it purports to be a crime fighting strategy, zero tolerance can all too easily become a manifestation of intolerance.

Also, despite early and apparently spectacular successes in New York, the evidence in support of zero tolerance is problematic. It is noted by a number of commentators that crime also fell in a number of US cities where zero tolerance was not practised. Bowling (1998), in one of the only academic studies so far undertaken in New York, concluded that the fall in the murder rate had more to do with the decline in the use of crack cocaine than it had to do with any policing strategy. In fact there was increasing disquiet in New York about policing tactics, which became focused when an unarmed young black man named Amado Diallo was shot and killed by four police officers in 1998.

The popularity of zero tolerance policing was only one manifestation of a significant move — begun in 1979, but which gathered pace in the 1990s — which was intended to re-focus policing on to the crime problem. Crime had been rising steadily during the 1970s, but this was also an era of increasing disorder, as industrial disputes had become confrontational and violent.

Increasing demand and increasing complexity — 'core business'

The 1970s were also characterised by increasing dissatisfaction among all ranks in the police service. Public sector pay restraint in the latter part of the decade had hit the service hard, recruitment was very difficult and morale was low. By 1978 the Police Staff Associations were mounting an assertive campaign for better pay and conditions, and increased resources generally for the service. During the run up to the 1979 General Election, both main political parties vied with each other with promises of increased funding. It was the Conservatives who made the most generous promises, and in the end their strong campaign on law and order played an important part in their election victory. In the early years the Government honoured its promises and the police service was the beneficiary in real terms of increases in resources, although the majority of the additional moneys were devoted to paying police officers.

However, it was not only resources that were increasing. The 1980s can be characterised as a period of dramatically increasing demands being made on the police service. Not only did the police have to cope with the problems of civil disorders in our cities and the 18-month long miners' strike, but crime rose steadily, as did calls for assistance from the public. All of which far outstripped the additional resources that the Government provided. The police response was effectively to abandon the idea of foot patrol in favour of mobile response by officers in cars. Even this was not enough, though, and senior officers soon realised that they had to develop ways to manage the demands that were being made upon the service. Their response was to begin to prioritise incidents and calls for assistance, and to focus on what became known as 'core business'. This new focus was no doubt welcomed by the Government, which was becoming increasingly irritated with the service for failing to stem the rising crime rate; but when John Major was returned to office in 1992, it soon became clear that the police were considered to be ripe for reform.

Kenneth Clarke, the new Home Secretary, set about the police with a will and commissioned a series of studies into policing. The Posen Inquiry (named after the senior Home Office civil servant who chaired it, but officially known as the 'Core and Ancillary Task Review') was intended to identify roles undertaken by the police which could either be abandoned, or taken on by some other agency thus freeing the service for its core duties. While the Review did not identify significant areas of work which could be shed, it did have a very significant effect and confirmed in the minds of many in the service that they could no longer attempt to fulfil all of the roles that the public demanded.

It was not only the police who had come to that conclusion. In 1993 the Government published a White Paper, *Police Reform: A Service for the Twenty-First Century* (Home Office, 1993). What was very clear was that the Government was determined not only to see the police operating under strict financial controls, but also that it saw the primary role of the police as the prevention and detection of crime. There is of course nothing new in that crime featured centrally in the instructions to the New Police in 1829 and has for long been regarded as the primary purpose of the police by junior officers. What was new, however, was the clear determination of the Conservatives in 1993 and New Labour when they came to power in 1997, to push through their reforms. The performance culture demanded by New Public Management now requires police forces to address key policy objectives set by the Home Secretary. Police forces, and even police areas or 'command units', are ranked against each other in league tables which are published, and pawed over in the Press and broadcast media.

Given all of this impetus to change, it would be surprising if policing were not substantially different in the year 2001 from what it had been in its previous 172 years. Policing is different: it is far more professional, and it is driven by the twin demands of increased efficiency and performance. More recently the Audit Commission, in a series of police papers, was critical of the way in which the service was organised and managed. In particular, two influential reports, *Streetwise* (1996a) and *Helping with Enquiries* (1993) made significant recommendations about uniform patrol and criminal investigation. The result has been that patrolling is now planned and targeted, while criminal investigation departments rely much more on analysing intelligence and targeting criminals than on investigating crimes once they have been committed, an approach known as 'intelligence led policing'.

Despite all of the evidence as to its ineffectiveness as a crime control technique, the police have again begun to patrol on foot. They do so not because it prevents or detects crime. Although the more systematic targetting of foot patrols following the publication in 1996 of *Streetwise* may have increased the effectiveness of the patrol function slightly. However, the principal impetus for the increased emphasis on uniformed patrol is mainly because the public like to see police officers in uniform. The police still respond quickly to incidents, but only those that they regard as urgent. If a situation is not regarded as requiring immediate action a response may be delayed, or the caller may be told that no officer will attend. The police still try to detect crime, although again they choose those crimes into which they will put their resources. The most common crimes, such as thefts from cars and what have become known as minor property offences, will most likely attract administrative effort by a civilian support worker rather than investigative effort by a police officer. The police will also attend the scene of a road accident, but only in the case of serious injury, major disruption to traffic, or allegations of intoxication or dangerous driving. The public, of course, know much of this and they seem to have accepted it. But there is evidence that they have not accepted it willingly, and they are now much more critical and much less supportive of the police than they were even ten years ago, and this ultimately will have an effect on policing.

The police on their own are ineffective at preventing crime. The Blair Government has acknowledged this by recognising that crime prevention can only be achieved by coordinating the activities of a range of organisations and individuals; and although they obviously have a great deal to contribute, experience has shown that the police are not the most appropriate organisation to undertake the coordinating role. Accordingly, the Crime and Disorder Act 1998 gives prime responsibility to local authorities, and requires the police and other statutory agencies to work together to produce effective strategies for preventing crime and disorder.

Research also tells us that the police are not very effective in detecting crime, although detection rates vary considerably according to the seriousness of the crime. This is largely the consequence of two factors: first, the resources that the police are likely to put into an investigation; and, secondly, in the case of serious crime at least, the fact that the offender is likely to be known to the victim and that, even when there are no witnesses, there is often sufficient evidence to identify the suspect relatively quickly. Nevertheless, the amount of crime detected by the police has fallen constantly over the years and now stands at less than 30 per cent of all recorded offences (Morgan and Newburn, 1997).

Detected or cleared crimes fall into two categories — primary and secondary detection. A primary detection is where the offender is arrested as a consequence of being 'caught in the act', or as a result of evidence gathered after the event. A secondary detection is where the police interview people after they have been charged with an offence, or after conviction and while they are serving a term of imprisonment. In these cases the police obtain an admission to further offences which can then be taken into consideration at the end of the trial or 'written off.' One of the principal reasons for the fall in detection rates over the years is not that the police have become less effective, as primary detections remain remarkably stable. It is because evidence of malpractice in obtaining secondary detections has led to a progressive tightening of the rules under which they are obtained, and a much more rigorous examination of the circumstances before they can be accepted.

In the case of primary detections, all of the evidence tells us that the police alone do not detect crimes. In most cases the offender is either detained at the scene by the victim or witnesses, or is identified as a result of being recognised or described by a witness. Whatever the circumstances, offenders are far more likely to be arrested by a uniformed officer responding to a call from a member of the public than by a detective investigating the crime after the event. This reliance on information provided by the public remains true today, despite the sophisticated technical aids that are now available to the police. Computers and forensic science are now essential aspects of criminal investigations, and the police have pinned a great deal of faith on the development of the national DNA database. We should not, however, over-estimate the potential of technology. After all, the police have had a national database of fingerprints for many years now, but only a very small percentage of crimes are ever detected by fingerprint evidence alone. Fingerprints, forensic science and DNA are essential to effective detection, but they invariably act to confirm evidence provided by witnesses or other traditional means of enquiry after a suspect has been identified, rather than identifying a suspect in the first instance. The clear message to the police, then, is that successful crime detection depends critically on the willingness of the general public to cooperate with them, and to provide evidence and information.

An emergency response organisation?

As we have established, policing was always about much more than crime and for many years the police performed a wide range of other tasks. Some of these were supervisory or licensing roles set out in legislation or regulations, but there were also a number of residual functions, most (if not all) of which had a social rather than a legal basis. We could ask, for example, why it is that the police will notify relatives in the case of a sudden death? Clearly, if the death has occurred in suspicious circumstances or in a accident that is being investigated, the police need evidence of identity and of any other relevent information, but why should they do it when requested (for example) by a hospital? The answer is quite straightforward. They do it because they have the infrastructure and they are available. As Punch and Naylor (1974) point out, the police have acquired these roles by virtue of their position as a 24-hour emergency response organisation. Waddington (1999) questions this analysis, however, and asks why it is that the police undertake some roles and not others. He argues that they do not repair broken down cars, or wake up students who have overslept on the day of an examination. But of course he is wrong. The police are not established to do either, but there are many examples of when they have done both. The police have always acted as an agency both of first and last resort: the first resort in an emergency and the last resort in a crisis. How many exhausted hitchhikers, for example, have found overnight shelter in a police station? None of this was done under any formal arrangements, and no doubt much of it would have been frowned upon, but that did not stop it taking place.

CONCLUSION

It is our contention that successful policing is about much more than targets and efficiency, and the recent desire to redefine policing in terms of crime and disorder misses the point because it has focused on what the police do, rather than on what policing is. The essence of successful policing in Britain is — and always has been — rooted in the extent to which the police can engage the active support of the public. In England and Wales policing has had a symbolic significance, and it is legitimate to raise concerns about the relentless drive for performance and targets. It is as yet too early to have a clear picture of the effect that the performance culture will have on the relationship between the police and the public, or what the knock-on effect will be on crime and crime detection, but it is perhaps instructive to examine some of the few pieces of evidence that we do have. The first relates directly to Britain, while the second relates to incidents in the United States.

In his report on the Brixton disorders of 1981, Lord Scarman noted that the police had lost contact with the public, and that this had played a contributory part in the development of suspicion and tension in the area which had eventually been ignited by the heavy handed and insensitive way in which a operation to combat street crime had been effected.

Similarly, in 1992, serious rioting broke out in Los Angeles following the acquittal of four police officers who had been accused of beating a black motorist. The verdict was surprising, because the whole incident had been captured on video and widely broadcast in the United States and elsewhere. In the aftermath of the riots a board of enquiry was set up to investigate the causes of the disturbances. In its report the board noted that over the years the Los Angeles Police Department had adopted a highly professional approach to policing, targeting crime and creating specialist task forces, which had resulted in an aggressive confrontational style backed by a wide range of performance indicators (Waddington, 1999). In effect the Los Angeles Police abandoned the notion of general patrol duties with a broadly and often ill-defined remit to main public safety, and substituted a much more narrow remit to control crime. Yet interestingly crime was not controlled; reported crime did not fall and clearance rates did not rise. What actually happened was that the public became hostile to the police and in effect withdrew their support.

That was Los Angeles, and we are not suggesting that the police in Britain are adopting the same tactics, although occasionally some within and outside of the police would like this to happen. The British police learned their lessons in the 1980s, and specialist squads of officers have generally been unfashionable in this country for a number of years. Here, the emphasis is to get officers back on the beat. There is, however, compelling evidence that significant sections of the community — and in particular the ethnic minority communities — feel distant and alienated from the police (see Chapter 6). The public like to see patrolling police officers because it makes them feel more confident; it reduces the fear of crime rather than the incidence of crime. But when a crime is committed the police need the public to help them solve it. If the adoption of the performance culture in Britain ultimately has the same effect as it did in Los Angeles, the police will lose that support.

There is no doubt that when serious crimes are committed the public will continue to respond when the police appeal for witnesses, especially as the police are seen as being supportive of the community which is being policed and appealed to. Media attention that surrounds the reconstruction of serious crimes will continue to illicit a response, and programmes like *Crimewatch* and the *Crime Squad* draw large audiences because there is a fascination with crime. Such programmes do sometimes jog people's memories, and they do result in guilty people being caught and convicted, but they feature the minority of cases deemed worthy of media exposure and effort. Notwithstanding all of that, there is evidence that the public are becoming disillusioned with the police and are increasing willing to take the law into their own hands. A recent study into the operation of a private security firm in the North of England revealed that residents were prepared to pay for private patrols of their neighbourhoods because they had lost confidence in the police, and the ex-criminals who were operating the patrols would not be constrained by legal niceties if they were to find anyone breaking into their homes (see Chapter 8). In another example, a farmer, Tony Martin, was convicted of murder when he shot and killed a teenage boy who had broken into his home. The publicity that followed suggested that there was considerable public support for the law on self-defence to be amended to allow people to defend their property rather more aggressively than is currently allowed. These are only two examples, but they should concern us because they illustrate a disillusionment and dissatisfaction with the police and the criminal justice system.

There is a paradox in policing, that increased efficiency does not necessarily result in increased effectiveness. We argue that the more efficient the police become the more they lose their symbolic significance, and as a direct consequence the support that they rely upon from the public gradually leeches away. It is not that the public withdraw cooperation in an active sense, but more that they cease to rely upon the police in times of crisis. They begin to view the police as irrelevant to their lives; the police become perceived as 'experts' equipped with a range of technical wizardry which can be utilised to solve crime. As a consequence, the public do not regard themselves as having a role to play. This is further compounded by a very real perception that victims and witnesses are treated badly by the remainder of the criminal justice system, and this has resulted in the unwillingness of ordinary people to 'get involved'.

The police should never be expected to separate fighting squirrels or to untangle knitting, but successful policing has much deeper foundations than the immediately and obviously measurable. Crime and disorder are problems for society as a whole, and the police are only one part of the solution.

3   Police Performance

INTRODUCTION

'The British police are the best in the world'. This is a well-worn cliché, but does it have any basis in fact? Sadly it is a question that is almost impossible to answer. Part of the problem is that the police perform such a wide variety of tasks, of which crime fighting is but one. The Association of Chief Police Officers (ACPO) estimates that in a full 24-hour period only 18 per cent of calls for help are about crime, and they take up approximately 30 per cent of police time. Nevertheless, this chapter will be almost entirely concerned with police performance in respect of crime. This is not merely because crime control is the single area of police activity that most exercises the public, but also because, ostensibly, it offers the widest range of performance measures. Whereas it is simply not possible to evaluate the police's effectiveness in, for example, attending a traffic accident, or helping a pensioner across the road, measures are available by which we can quantify both the level of crime and the rate at which it is solved. However, we will argue that these measures must be treated with extreme caution and, more importantly, that policing is neither the cause of nor the solution to the crime problem.

THE CRIME RATE

Methods of measurement

There are two main measures of the crime rate. The first is the crime figures recorded by the police; and the second is the British Crime

Survey (BCS). Whereas the former has been compiled, in one form or another, since 1837, and tend to be referred to as the official crime figures, the BCS was begun only in 1982 and is, in effect, a victim survey conducted by the Home Office on a random sample of the population aged 16 and over, about offences they have experienced in the previous year. Because it includes those crimes not reported to the police, the BCS is generally seen as providing a more accurate picture and can be used in comparison with the recorded crime figures to reveal what is known as 'hidden crime'. The BCS often paints a picture at odds with that drawn by the use of other statistical measures of crime by revealing, for example, that people from ethnic minorities are more likely to be the victims, rather than the perpetrators, of crime (Coleman and Moynihan, 1996).

The rise in crime

Both the recorded crime figures and the BCS suggest that Britain's crime problem has steadily grown. Notwithstanding the occasional annual fall, the level of recorded crime in England and Wales has risen by an average of 5.1 per cent a year since 1918. Over the last two decades the rises have been especially sharp. In 1979 there were around 2.4 million crimes recorded in England and Wales, but by 1992 that figure had reached over 5.4 million. From 1994 onwards there were annual falls, but in the year up to September 1999 it rose by 2.2 per cent to 5.23 million, the first rise in five years. In fact the headline figure grew by 14 per cent in the year up to March 1999, but the rise was entirely due to new calculation methods introduced by the Home Office more accurately to reflect the number of victims of crime. The reasons for the introduction of these new methods are discussed later in this chapter. There was a further rise of 3.8 per cent during the year ending March 2000, bringing the total number of recorded offences to 5.3 million (*Daily Telegraph*, 18 July 2000).

Property offences make up around three-quarters of all recorded crime, with vehicle crime accounting for about 28 per cent of the total, burglary 24 per cent and other theft 23 per cent. Violent crimes make up only around 6 per cent of the total, and of these, only a small proportion involve serious violence. It should also be remembered that some fluctuations in the crime rate can be due to changes in the definition of crime. For example, before April 1998 credit card fraud was recorded only if reported; but since then, if a police investigation uncovers fraud it will be recorded regardless of whether or not it has been reported. From the same date minor cases of criminal damage, valued at under £20, were also recorded.

The recorded crime figures contain significant geographical variations. More crimes tend to be committed in poorer, urban areas than in rural areas, but there can be significant variations between apparently similar areas. For example, in the year ending March 2000 the robbery rate in Manchester was six times and the car theft rate twice that of Sheffield, a similar sized city only 40 miles away (*Daily Telegraph*, 18 July 2000).

The BCS has consistently painted a far bleaker picture than the recorded crime figures. The seven surveys so far published have suggested that at most only half of known crime is reported, a figure which has progressively shrunk and may be as low as a quarter (Muncie, 1996, at 22–23). And whereas the recorded crime figures showed a drop of around 4 per cent between 1991 and 1995, the BCS suggested that there had been a rise of 23 per cent. The survey conducted in 1998 for the first time recorded a drop in crime in nearly all the offences that the BCS measures. Thus it revealed that there had been a 7 per cent drop in burglary, a 17 per cent drop in crimes of violence, and a 25 per cent drop in thefts from vehicles (Home Office Research and Statistics Department, 1998). Despite these figures, the Home Office predicted that property crimes would increase again in 2000 and 2001 (*Sunday Times*, 15 August 1999).

THE POLICE CLEAR-UP RATE

Like the crime figures, the statistics recording the rate at which police forces catch criminals — the so-called clear-up rate — also make depressing reading. In 1980 the clear-up rate for England and Wales was 40 per cent, but by 1994 it had fallen to less than 25 per cent (*Guardian*, 31 January 1994). A 1998 report by the Audit Commission revealed that the police fail to solve as many as 92 per cent of burglaries, and that less than half of all street robberies — so-called muggings — and violent assaults result in convictions or arrest (*Sunday Times*, 21 June 1998).

The detection rates for more serious crimes are far better, indeed they have remained consistently high. Murders increased from 624 in 1984 to 681 in 1996, with the detection rate falling only slightly, from 96 per cent to 93 per cent over the same period. Similarly, kidnappings trebled to 1,429, but the detection rate was also high at 81 per cent. Reported rapes doubled from 2,855 in 1988 to 5,759 in 1996, with detection increasing from 72 per cent to 77 per cent.

Home Office statistics show huge variations between various forces. The percentage of all crime solved by direct investigation in 1998/9 was 29 per cent, but ranged from 69 per cent in Dyffed Powys to 28 per cent in the West Midlands. Dyffed-Powys also headed the league tables for the clear-up rates for violent crimes and burglaries in 1997/8, with figures of 92 per cent and 32 per cent respectively. The West Midlands again came bottom of the violent crime league table with a clear-up rate of 42 per cent, and Leicestershire was bottom of the burglary clear-up table with just 8 per cent. The number of crimes solved by direct investigation annually per officer averaged 9.4, but again varied hugely across different force areas, from 15.5 in Gwent to 5.5 in Surrey (*Sunday Times*, 21 June 1998).

An Audit Commission survey published in 1999 showed similarly dramatic variations in other performance measures. Detection rates per officer varied from 16 in Gwent to 6.4 in Surrey; the percentage of time spent in contact with the public varied from 79 per cent in Durham to 41 per cent in Hertfordshire; and primary detection rates varied from 16 per officers annually in Gwent to 6.4 in Surrey (Audit Commission, 1999). While the clear-up rate declined, the number of reported incidents that the police had to deal with rose by 2 per cent between 1993/4 and 1997/8. The number of police 999 calls rose 38 per cent to 7.3 million over the same period, a phenomenon that can be largely attributed to the proliferation of mobile phones (HM Inspectorate of Constabulary, 1998).

THE INCREASE IN POLICE RESOURCES

Crime rates may have risen and clear-up rates fallen, but the Governments of the past 20 years cannot be accused of having starved the police of resources. The police are by far the most expensive component of the criminal justice system. In 1995/6, annual spending on the criminal justice system, which also includes the Prison Service, the Lord Chancellor's Department, the Probation Service, the magistrates' courts, the Crown Prosecution Service, Legal Aid and the Criminal Injuries Compensation Scheme, was £10.5 billion, of which almost two-thirds (£6.6 billion) were spent on the police. Between 1979 and the early 1990s budgets rose in real terms by almost 90 per cent, and by 1998 total expenditure on the police stood at £7.21 billion. Of this, £3.95 billion was accounted for by officers' salaries and a further £1.02 billion by civilian staff costs. £830 million was spent on staff pensions, a figure that is set to rise steeply as increasing numbers of officers retire and live longer (Morgan and Newburn, 1997). Police numbers rose steadily to a peak of 128,290 in March 1993, then fell back to 124,418 by March 2000 (*Daily Telegraph*, 31 August 2000).

In 1987/8, policing in England and Wales cost £67 annually per head of population. A decade on this had risen to £123.10 (HM Inspectorate of Constabulary, 1998). As with the clear-up rate, there are wide variations between the costs in different force areas. The Metropolitan Police were by far the most expensive at £215, with Merseyside a distant second at £152. Suffolk, North Yorkshire and Surrey were the cheapest at £95 (*Sunday Times*, 21 June 1998).

POLICING AND CRIME

The bald facts appear to show that police performance has been in serious decline for decades: despite huge increases in resources, crime levels have continued their inexorable rise and detection rates have fallen. But can we really blame rising crime on failures of policing?

In reality the causes of crime are complex, many layered and shifting. A relatively simple analysis was set out by Professor Robert Reiner of the London School of Economics, one of the country's leading criminologists:

> ... for a crime to occur four ingredients are necessary: motive, means, opportunity and lack of control. There must be a motivated offender with the means to commit the crime, the opportunity presented by a vulnerable victim, and the offence must not be prevented by either external controls — police security, etc. — or internalised controls, i.e., conscience — what the psychologist Hans Eysenck graphically called the 'inner policeman'. (Reiner, 1994, at 10–17)

It has been argued that the rising crime rate is the result of the police having steadily become more ineffective and thereby reducing significantly what Reiner terms the 'external controls' on criminals. For example, the declining use of stop and search by the Metropolitan Police in the wake of the Macpherson Report on the Stephen Lawrence case (see Chapter 6) was blamed by the Conservative opposition and the Police Federation, among others, for a 30 per cent annual rise in robberies. This argument appeared to be borne out by a report 'Searches in London' (see also Chapter 6) prepared for the Metropolitan Police by a former Home Office researcher (*Guardian*, 16 December 1999). However the statistician on whose analysis the claim was based, protested that it represented a complete misrepresentation of his findings (Dr Jeremy Penzer, letter to the *Guardian*, 17 December 1999).

Far more profound social factors than policing are generally behind the rising crime rate. For example, since 10 to 24-year-old males traditionally commit most crime (Wilson and Ashton, 1998), a demographic fluctuation involving a rise in their numbers will tend to increase crime levels. This was one of the factors that caused the Home Office to predict a surge in crime during 2000 and 2001. A further factor is rising consumer spending, which means that more goods are available to steal. New technologies can also fuel crime. Greater use of the Internet, for example, was one of the main factors behind the 29 per cent rise in fraud in 1999.

It is our view that by far the greatest factor contributing to a rise in the crime rate in recent years has been the growth of poverty. According to the Joseph Rowntree Foundation's *Breadline Britain* study, the proportion of households living in poverty grew from 14 per cent in 1983 to 24 per cent in 1999 (Joseph Rowntree Foundation, 2000). Academic studies have consistently shown that there are 14 million people in Britain living in poverty, and over the past two decades they have grown steadily poorer. Between 1979 and 1993 the wealthiest 10 per cent of people in Britain had become on average 65 per cent richer; but the poorest 10 per cent were, on average, around 14 per cent poorer, a real terms drop in their weekly income of £11. Among the poorest 20 per cent of the population (around 11 million people), couples with children were approximately £9 a week worse off, and single people with children were £26 per week worse off (Joseph Rowntree Foundation, 2000).

The doubling of the recorded crime rate between 1979 and 1993 was accompanied by a similar rise in unemployment. The number of people living in a household with no wage earner rose from one in 12 in 1979 to one in five by the mid-1990s. A United Nations study discovered that the average income in Britain in the mid–1990s was £11,096, but that the poorest 20 per cent of the population were receiving only £2,548, which made them only marginally better off than their counterparts in Hungary. According to the Organisation for Economic Cooperation and Development, over the previous two decades Britain had the worst poverty record in the Western World (*Guardian*, 12 January 2000).

Of course, not all poor people turn to crime, but the National Child Development Study, which followed the lives of 17,000 people born in 1958, found a clear link between poverty and 'deviant' behaviour (which was defined as 'disorders of emotion or conduct'). A 1995 study by the Government's Office of Population, Censuses and Surveys found that 7 per cent of three-year-olds brought up in poor inner city areas already showed signs of moderate or severe behavioural problems, and the percentage grew among older children. In the same year a study of 18- to 34-year-olds by the Demos think tank found that more than a third felt alienated and outside 'the system', and derived a sense of pride from flouting its rules.

In the face of the profound social breakdown that has affected Britain over the past two decades, the police stand little or no chance of making a significant impact on crime. This is one journalist's account of the uphill struggle faced by the police in Hyde Park, a poor, inner-city district of Leeds:

The police, from Milgarth division, had once used a team of fourteen community constables to patrol their area, including Hyde Park, on foot. But during the year before the children burned down the Jolly Brewer [pub], this system collapsed. The patrolling constables were uncovering so much crime that they were drowning in work. The division pulled them back and renamed them 'beat managers'. This had two advantages: it stopped them uncovering so much crime, which made the crime figures look slightly better; and it allowed them to form teams to target particular kinds of crime in the hope of making arrests. They dressed in plain clothes and took bicycles to mount mobile ambushes on joy riders who tried to steal the cars that the commuters left behind them every morning. They lay in wait outside the old grammar school on the eastern edge of Hyde Park, where wealthy parents paid thousands of pounds to educate their children privately and where the children had discovered that a school cap was as good as a banner marked 'mug me'. They got some results but the truth was that, caught between the plague of crime in Hyde Park and the shortage of officers, the police were fighting a losing battle. (Davies, 1997)

Nevertheless, right-wing politicians and theoreticians who shaped the political landscape of the past two decades provided a very different explanation for the growing crime rate. Citing the fact that the growth of welfare benefits and prosperity between the end of the War and the 1970s was accompanied by a growth in crime, they argued that the welfare state had created a comfortable safety net, which sapped the moral fibre of its recipients and thereby created a feckless and irresponsible society (Murray, 1984). But the rise in crime during the heyday of the welfare state might be equally well explained by the simple fact that the general increase in prosperity over this period meant that there were many more attractive goods, such as cars, televisions and hi-fis, to steal. The fact that crime also grew during the 1980s and 1990s, when welfare benefits continued to be cut and joblessness remained consistently high, the New Right argued, was due variously to the enduring welfare mindset, the failure to pare back benefits far enough, and the failure of the criminal justice system to deal sufficiently harshly with offenders.

This analysis conveniently ignored the experience of countries such as Germany and France, which during the 1980s and 1990s largely maintained economic and social policies designed to redistribute wealth and protect the poorest members of society. Neither of those countries has been immune from substantial crime problems, but in Germany the recorded crime rate rose only slightly and in France it actually fell. In the wake of major urban riots in 1981, the Government of the Socialist President François Mitterand recognised that unless the problems of the poorest communities were tackled head-on, the crime problem could spiral out of control. It launched a substantial programme of social investment with the concept of 'social crime prevention' at its core. When the riots occurred the recorded annual crime figure in France was 3.5 million, which was roughly the same as for England and Wales. By the end of the 1980s it had fallen to about 3 million, compared with the increase to 5.5 million in England and Wales (Wilson and Ashton, 1998, at 157).

Can policing affect crime?

The obvious answer to this question remains 'Yes'; but as we have seen, huge real terms increases in government spending on the police have failed to prevent the relentless rise in crime. In exploring the issue it is helpful again to compare some of the statistics for different forces: three times fewer crimes are solved by direct investigation in the West Midlands than in Dyffed Powys; the violent crime rate is about three times higher in Humberside than in Surrey; and policing is twice as expensive for the citizens of London than it is for the people of Surrey. These figures are, in part, a reflection of the fact that the West Midlands, Humberside and the Metropolitan Police serve large conurbations, whereas Dyffed Powys, Surrey and Suffolk are either more rural, more prosperous, or both. Since they do not face the same problems as those exercising the large conurbations, rural and shire forces have the twin advantages of fewer strains on their finances and more time to dedicate officers to clearing up crime. A study by the Audit Commission (1990) discovered that, even when such variations were taken into account, some forces appeared to perform significantly better than others. Variations in social conditions cannot explain why, for example, primary detection rates and detection rates per officer are so much lower in affluent Surrey than in relatively poor Gwent.

There is a widely held assumption that crime reductions can be achieved by increasing police resources and hiring more officers, and police spending and manpower remain key measures of politicians' commitment to law and order. However, the available evidence suggests that police numbers do not affect the crime rate. An Audit Commission survey published in 1999 established that improved clear-up rates were not connected with increased spending. Of the four forces which received the highest percentage budget increases — Cheshire, Durham, South Wales and South Yorkshire — only South Yorkshire improved its rate of detection. The Commission also found that increasing the numbers of officers did not necessarily affect the crime rate, its 1999 Annual Report on the Police and Fire Services noting that, 'In some forces there were increases in the number of officers per 1,000 of population, but the percentage of crimes solved either stayed the same or fell'.

Other statistics bear out the Audit Commission's findings. In the four years from 1990 to 1993 inclusive, there were annual rises in the number of officers of between 0.1 per cent and 0.9 per cent, but over the same period the number of notifiable offences rose annually by between 4 and 18 per cent. In all but one of the next six years the number of police officers fell by between 0.3 and 0.6 per cent, but crime levels fell in all those years by between 0.1 and 5 per cent. Nevertheless, staff levels affect the police's ability to respond to crime. When in 2000 Metropolitan Police numbers fell to a 20-year low of 25,400, down from 28,400 a decade earlier (*Daily Telegraph*, 16 June 2000) insiders claimed the force was unable to attend all 999 calls and that shoplifters caught by security staff were being allowed to go free (*Sunday Telegraph*, 2 April 2000).

If more officers do not affect the crime rate, what about the way in which they are deployed? It is often argued that police performance would be improved not by increasing the numbers of officers, but by ensuring that more officers spent more time in 'front line' crime fighting duties. Research into the work patterns of CID officers has shown that only 40 to 45 per cent of their work is spent investigating crime, with the rest being spent report writing, attending court, taking refreshments and on miscellaneous duties (Burrows and Tarling, 1982). Uniformed constables spend even less time at what the public might consider to be the 'coal face' of crime fighting. Home Office research (Burrows and Tarling, 1982) has shown that factors such as sick leave, the shift system, holidays, training, paper work and time spent interviewing prisoners, meant that police officers spend only between a half and two-thirds of their time outside the police station. Of the time spent outside the office, only a third is spent actually patrolling.

Sick leave is a particular problem. In 1998 the Home Office discovered that officers took an average of 12 days a year off sick at an annual cost of £210 million. An earlier study of the Metropolitan Police established that the average rate of sick leave per officer was even higher, at three weeks a year. Prompted by concern that officers were abusing sick leave, Home Secretary Jack Straw gave David O'Dowd, HM Chief Inspector of Constabulary, his full blessing to take greater steps to tackle the issue. At the same time Mr Straw announced that police forces would be able to keep any money they could save by cutting the number of officers retiring early on medical grounds. When Mr Straw came to office he set a target for police forces to reduce medical retirements to 33 per cent, but figures published the following year, while showing a slight improvement, revealed that such retirements were still over 50 per cent in some forces, and ran as high as 65 per cent in Derbyshire. This was more than three times as many as in the best performing force (Surrey), which had a figure of just 18 per cent (*Sunday Telegraph*, 26 July 1998). Home Office figures released in 2000 showed that the sick rate leave was continuing to rise in some forces, including Derbyshire, North Yorkshire and Gloucestershire. However, by targetting sick leave abuses, the Metropolitan Police were able to save £23 million in 1999.

A clamp-down on sick leave coupled with administrative reorganisation might result in more bobbies on the beat, but would it help in the fight against crime? As we have argued in Chapter 2, while many people undoubtedly feel safer if they know that a police officer is nearby, the available evidence suggests that it makes no difference to the crime clear-up figures. Yet many British forces have launched high-profile campaigns against certain types of offenders — for example, the Metropolitan Police's 1993 Operation Bumble Bee targeted burglars — and Operation Eagle Eye two years later focused on muggers. These operations aimed resources against alleged persistent offenders and towards improved intelligence networks and surveillance technologies. But more proactive and interventionist policing does not necessarily lead to more arrests. Home Office statistics show that the number of recorded stops and searches by the police in England and Wales leapt between 1986 and 1994, from 110,000 to 576,000, but over the same period the percentage of those that led to arrests fell from 17.2 per cent to 12 per cent (Wilkins and Hayward, 2001). Arguably, the increased use of stop and search would have undermined the fight against crime by alienating many innocent citizens from the police.

Other innovations intended to improve efficiency also had unforeseen adverse consequences. For example, the decision to put officers in vehicles erected a barrier between the police and the community and meant that officers and local people were unable to familiarise themselves with each other. This in turn made it more difficult to establish a bond of trust so that the police became alienated from the public, and in areas of social strife this alienation often gave way to resentment. In turn, the public were less likely to provide the police with information that would help in the fight against crime.

'LIES, DAMN LIES AND STATISTICS'

There are few areas of human endeavour to which Mark Twain's aphorism is more appropriately applied than the evaluation of police performance. Take that most fundamental of statistics — the crime rate. When we think of crime we usually think of burglary, auto theft, robbery, assault and murder, rather than corporate crime, tax evasion and fraud, but crime is constantly evolving and developing. Behaviour which had previously been seen as 'criminal' can become lawful, such as consenting homosexual behaviour between 18-year-olds. Equally, previously legal activities, such as not wearing a seat belt in a car or a crash helmet on a motorbike, have become illegal.

The 1980s and 1990s in particular saw new crimes invented for specific groups, or behaviour associated with those groups targeted by successive governments. For example, laws have been passed against joy riders, squatters, hunt saboteurs, and New Age travellers. All of this makes some of the certainties about crime of which we have been assured more difficult to sustain. If crimes can be abolished or invented, how can we tell if crime in Britain is getting better or worse? How can we tell if crime is rising or falling if it is impossible to find an accurate definition of what it is that we are attempting to measure?

As we have seen, there are two main measures of the crime rate — the recorded crime figures and the BCS, which is a study of victims. Both these measures have fundamental flaws. Indeed, no less a figure than the Editor of the Home Office's official digest of information on the criminal justice system, commented that 'no one knows the true extent of crime in this country. Two main measures are available but each, in its own way, may not accurately record the scale of crime' (Home Office Research and Statistics Department, 1995). The main problem with the recorded crime figures is that, for a variety of reasons, some crimes go unreported. For example, victims might regard the crime committed against them as too trivial to report, or believe that they might not be treated sympathetically or seriously by the police. Other crimes, such as tax evasion, which is recorded by the Inland Revenue, or VAT evasion, which is recorded by Customs and Excise, will appear in official criminal statistics only if the perpetrator is subsequently brought to court. It could be argued that the economic damage created by these offences is far more damaging than that caused by those offences against property which make up the bulk of our official statistics, and yet it is rare for them to appear in official accounts of crime in our country. Alternatively, the increase in crime might also reflect merely an increased reporting of crime. For example, a nationwide anti-burglary campaign was mounted in 1982, partly in response to a 50 per cent increase in the number of recorded burglaries between 1971 and 1981. Yet information from other sources suggests that there was almost no change in the rate of burglary at all, and that the increase in the amount of reported and subsequent recording of burglary can be accounted for by the greater availability of 'new for old' insurance policies, which produced an incentive for increased claims (Bottomley and Pease, 1986).

Other factors might also affect the extent of recorded crime. For example, the number of reported incidents of criminal damage shot up from 17,000 in 1969 to 124,000 in 1977. Until April 1998, criminal damage was officially defined as damage exceeding £20 in value, so the 'increase' prior to that date could have been largely due to inflation moving trivial incidents of damage into a more serious category of crime, rather than to an increased level of vandalism (*The New Statesman*, 22 January 1982).

The accuracy of the recorded crime figures also depends on the honesty of the officers who record them. There is an incentive for officers to play down the crime problem in their patch, because the less crime that is seen to be occurring there, the more effective they appear to be. Unfortunately this has led some officers to attempt to manipulate the crime figures. The favoured method in relation to crime rates is known in police slang as 'cuffing', because the crimes in effect disappear, as if secreted up the cuffs of the officer's uniform. The technique simply involves the non-recording of certain crimes. For example, an attempted burglary which causes damage of less than a certain amount might be reclassified as minor damage. Under Home Office rules an attempted burglary should be recorded as a crime, but once reclassified as minor damage it need not be. Another example is attempted car theft, which could be reclassified as vehicle interference, which is not a notifiable offence. Stolen handbags and wallets could also be removed from the statistics by being recorded as lost property, unless there was clear evidence of a thief at work. Violent crimes could also disappear from the statistics. For example, the notifiable offence of assault occasioning actual bodily harm (ABH) could be recorded as common assault, a minor offence which does not have to be recorded as a crime. Another method of cuffing is to treat a series of crimes in the same area by the same offender as a single offence. Thus a string of break-ins in the same block of flats over the course of an afternoon might be recorded as one offence.

The crime clear-up figures should also be treated with caution. Some offenders are more easily caught than others, for example vagrants, but are less of a problem to the community than those who are more difficult to apprehend, such as burglars or car thieves. It is possible to boost the clear-up rate by targeting vagrants, but for the number of undetected burglaries to rise. The net result is improved statistics but a less happy public.

Particular care must also be taken to distinguish between primary clear-up rates, based on actual charges and cautions, and secondary ones, based on prison visits and offenders asking for other offences to be taken into consideration ('TIC'). For many years these 'TICs' or 'write offs' have been an important, if questionable, element of CID tradecraft in all police forces. Both offender and detective benefit from this arrangement: the offender is looked upon more favourably by the courts and parole boards, and usually serves a shorter sentence than he might otherwise have done; and the detective's clear-up rate improves. Unfortunately, in many cases TICs are no more than a statistical sleight of hand.

Such dubious professional secrets have only rarely come to light. One of the most infamous instances was in 1986, when PC Ron Walker of the Kent police alleged that scores of detectives in the force were routinely fabricating crime figures by persuading convicted criminals to confess to hundreds of crimes they had not committed. This made the force's crime clear-up rates look considerably better than they would otherwise have done — in some parts of the county they were twice the national average (*The Observer*, 24 September 1989).

Performance targets and league tables

Since Ron Walker's day, the incentives to manipulate crime and performance figures have increased considerably. In the early 1990s the declining crime clear-up rate, set against the background of steady real terms increases in police budgets, prompted the Conservative Government to initiate a series of investigations into police organisation and performance. The studies were conducted by the Audit Commission, the National Audit Office and (most controversially) by Sir Patrick Sheehy, who was then chairman of the tobacco multinational BAT Industries.

Sheehy and others variously pinpointed that the police lacked effective managerial structures and goals, and recommended root and branch reforms. The police, by and large, resented the outsider's intrusive eye and vigorously protested that economies could not be made without the public paying the price of higher crime rates and lower clear-up rates. But senior officers soon came to realise that all other major areas of state expenditure were under scrutiny and whether they liked it or not they had to compete for finance. Some of the proposals were incorporated into the Police and Magistrates' Courts Act 1994, but this was nevertheless passed only after a heated public debate and a watering down of some of the more radical provisions.

One of the 1994 Act's most important innovations was the introduction of so-called key performance indicators and league tables. From April 1995 onwards, the Home Secretary laid down key performance indicators, such as clear-up rates for various categories of crime and response times to 999 calls, and published annual league tables which demonstrated how each force was performing. For their part, chief constables and their new streamlined police authorities were responsible for producing annual local police plans which set crime control targets, objectives and expenditure. The new measures vastly increased the pressure on the police to cut crime rates and improve the clear-up statistics. (See Figure 3.1 related to the Annual Policing Plan for the West Midlands.)

Performance Indicators and Targets

Reduction Indicators		Target %
Level of total crime		4
Level of vehicle crime		4
Level of burglary dwelling		5
Level of street robbery		4
Repeat victims of domestic burglary		10
Repeat victims of domestic violence		23
RTAs where lives are lost/serious injury		5
Detection Indicators		
a. All controlled drugs		1,200
b. Those involving heroin		250
Increase crimes detected by primary detections		33
No of crimes detected by primary detection by each officer		14
No of serious assaults and woundings detected by primary detection		80

Figure 3.1   Annual Policing Plan for the West Midlands, 1999–2000

A 1999 Report by the Audit Commission revealed evidence that forces systematically under-report the true extent of crime figures. Among the methods used were: (i) classifying multiple burglaries, for example in a block of flats in one day, as a single incident; (ii) recording multiple credit card frauds as a single offence; and (iii) excluding drug offences in which the offender is cautioned rather than charged. Indeed, official concern at the level of statistical manipulation prompted the Audit Commission and HM Inspectorate of Constabulary to change the way in which the police are allowed to collate their crime and detection figures. It was predicted that the new figures would show that large metropolitan forces, which have a greater proportion of officers to local population, were doing even worse than expected. Horrified by the manipulation of statistics, a Deputy Chief Constable of one force, who asked not to be named, accused senior officers of having 'under-estimated crime to make their figures look better' (*Sunday Times*, 21 June 1998).

HM Inspectorate of Constabulary's first in-depth analysis of crime reporting practices in England and Wales was published in 2000 and confirmed that under-recording was rife. The Report, entitled *On the Record*, found that 24 per cent of allegations received from the public did not make the crime statistics. Although the Government promised to review recording procedures in the light of these findings (*Daily Telegraph*, 1 August 2000), it appeared undeterred by the possible adverse effects of performance culture. In 2000, Home Secretary Jack Straw announced that forces would be set individual targets to reduce burglary and car crime, with a view to cutting the former by 25 per cent and the latter by 30 per cent by 2005. Five large urban forces (the Metropolitan Police, West Yorkshire, Merseyside, West Midlands and Greater Manchester) were also ordered to produce targets for reducing robberies.

One force shown to have been manipulating crime figures since the introduction of league tables was Nottinghamshire (see *Guardian*, 18 March 1999 and *Dispatches*, 18 March 1999). As with the Ron Walker case a decade earlier, the abuses came to light only through the actions of a brave whistle blower. Detective Superintendent Peter Coles, head of the force's Major Crimes Unit, was so appalled by the abuses he witnessed that he presented the force's senior officers with a lengthy memorandum entitled 'Ethics of Crime and Crime Investigation'. The document did not mince words. Coles warned his superiors:

> A culture of good results is burgeoning, paying scant regard to the methods employed by junior officers to serve the ambition of their seniors . . . the greatest danger is that we appear to believe in our own publicity and accept the hypocrisy as the truth. Rightly or wrongly, top management believe they are promoted upon performance, never mind whether the results measured are true or false.

Coles resigned from the force and filed a complaint against the chief constable, his deputy and two assistants.

The complaint was eventually investigated on behalf of the Police Complaints Authority by Bedfordshire police. The inquiry's findings were startling. It showed that in the mid-1990s, three of Nottigham-shire's nine divisions deliberately manipulated the force's computerised recording system in order to stop crimes showing up on the computer. Officially each crime was to be assigned a number, but by adding the letters T, I or N to that number the crime would not be recorded. To the outside world the force appeared to be performing well, with recorded crimes falling by 7,788 in 1996. Over 9,000 incidents recorded in the alternative systems did not show up in the force's official crime statistics. The report of the Bedfordshire inquiry stated that the 'vast majority' of those 9,000 plus entries 'were crimes and should have been recorded as such'. In other words, the fall in recorded crime of 7,700 was a complete fiction and the true figure may even have increased.

Nottinghamshire Constabulary was also at the forefront of massaging clear-up figures through so-called TICs, or write offs. Of the total number of crimes which the force claimed to have cleared up in 1996, 14 per cent — almost 5,300 offences — were write offs by prisoners. In the Arnold Division, prison write offs accounted for 30 per cent of cleared up crimes. Visits by detectives to prisoners are supposed to take place within strict guidelines laid down by the Home Office and HM's Inspectorate of Constabulary. Their purpose should be to gather intelligence and information, not to gain write offs, and, in all but exceptional circumstances, the prisoners are not supposed to be taken out of the prison. The Bedfordshire investigation revealed that 98 per cent of the prisoners whose files they examined had been taken out for the day. In most cases they were taken in a police car and asked to point out the houses or the premises they had burgled, a procedure known as 'nodding' because the prisoner customarily nods at the building he claims to have burgled.

One of the examples uncovered by the Bedfordshire inquiry into Nottinghamshire police was of a pair of shoplifters who were persuaded to write off 150 offences as TICs. They had told the police that, for practical reasons, they never stole on Thursdays or Sundays, yet 28 of the TICs were committed on those days. The Bedfordshire police discovered not only cases in which the offender had not committed the TICs that had been written off, but also that in some cases the offence which the offender had asked to be taken into consideration never happened in the first place. One man admitted to 37 burglaries, five of which were committed against people who insisted that they had never been burgled and a further five of which had taken place when he was locked up in prison. So keen were the Nottinghamshire police to improve their clear-up figures that an 11-year-old girl was persuaded to write off 80 shoplifting offences. A few months later a 10-year-old boy who had been caught stealing sweets was persuaded to write off 71 shoplifting offences. In each case the details of the offences were provided by the police, rather than by the supposed child offenders.

The Bedfordshire inquiry concluded that the abuses were not confined to a few errant individuals but were institutional. Indeed, the officer who persuaded the 10-year-old boy to agree to the write offs thought he was acting in accordance with force policy. When the Bedfordshire team investigated the force's central division in Nottingham they discovered that 91 per cent of TICs broke the rules. An internal audit by Nottinghamshire police of the Mansfield Division discovered that 48 per cent of TICs were unreliable. Among them, an incredible 95 per cent of shoplifting TICs had never been reported by their victims.

The force's own rules created another major loophole, allowing officers to improve the crime clear-up rate without actually solving crimes. The Home Office permits some crimes to be recorded as solved even if no conviction results from the police action. For example, if the defendant or vital prosecution witnesses die before the case comes to court. The crimes are given the heading 'Detected No Further Police Action' and are therefore known as DNFPAs. The Home Office requires that, in order for crimes to be classified as DNFPA, there must be enough evidence to bring the charge, but this condition was omitted from Nottinghamshire's rules, allowing the force to claim a very high clear-up rate for certain crimes, in particular sex offences. The clear-up rate for rape in 1996 was an ostensibly impressive 98.6 per cent, but the Bedfordshire team discovered that, force-wide, 60 per cent of these charges would not stand up. The figure for indecent assault was even higher, at 75 per cent.

Exposing his force's cheating cost Superintendent Peter Coles dear. Prior to his resignation, the force's senior command ordered that every copy of his memorandum of complaint should be seized and the original erased from the force computer. They even considered taking him to court and seeking an injunction if he attempted to leak the contents of the memorandum outside the force. A meeting at which the memorandum was due to be discussed was cancelled and Coles was removed from the force's Drug Strategy Group. Perhaps the most worrying aspect of the Nottinghamshire abuses is that they might not have come to light were it not for the principled stand of a brave officer. The Bedfordshire inquiry found no evidence of corruption; rather, the force's senior command set targets then failed to ensure that they were reached in an ethical manner.

The political context

Nationally, in 1997 official records showed a record drop of over 440,000 in recorded crime figures, which was around 9 per cent. The political significance of these figures cannot be overestimated, as they appeared to be a vindication of the hard-line criminal justice polices introduced a few years earlier by Conservative Home Secretary Michael Howard. Over the previous decades the criminal justice policy orthodoxy followed by Conservative and Labour Governments alike was that prison should be a last resort for persistent offenders because it tended, in the words of Conservative Home Secretary David Waddington in 1990, to be 'An expensive way of making bad people worse.' Yet to the delight of the 1993 Conservative Party Conference, Michael Howard broke with tradition, announcing that 'prison works' and promising a range of policies designed to 'get tough' with criminals. Among the most significant pieces of new legislation was the Crime (Sentences) Act 1997, which was voted through Parliament, with Labour support, shortly before that year's General Election. The Act introduced mandatory minimum sentences for certain categories of repeat offenders and abolished prisoners' rights to automatic remission.

The 'prison works' philosophy was a direct import from the United States, where its advocates, like the influential right-wing sociologist Charles Murray, argued that increasing crime figures could be attributed to the fact that falling rates of apprehension provided criminals with an incentive to commit crime. Sending more people to prison for longer would not only keep criminals off the street, but would also serve as a deterrent to potential criminals.

The steady fall in recorded crime from 1993 onwards was hailed by Conservatives as a vindication of Howard's policies, which saw the prison population increase by 50 per cent, to over 60,000 between 1993 and 1997. In fact the falling crime rate was more likely a function of the economic up-turn of the mid-1990s, which is likely to have resulted in fewer property crimes. Crucially, it may also have been a result of the introduction of police performance league tables, which gave police forces an incentive to massage the figures downwards.

No doubt the falling crime figures were one of the reasons the Labour Party leadership took the tactical decision to not oppose the Crime (Sentences) Act 1997. Nevertheless, the new Labour Home Secretary Jack Straw was only too aware of these statistical abuses when he took office in May 1997, and so he ordered new rules which would make previously non-notifiable offences notifiable once more. The new rules, which took effect from April 1998, were one of the main factors behind the large increase in the crime figures over the following 12 months.

CONCLUSION

There is nothing to say that abuses similar to those highlighted by the Bedfordshire inquiry into the Nottighamshire police have not taken place in other forces. They may have remained concealed because very few police insiders have the courage to 'blow the whistle'. According to HM's Inspectorate of Constabulary, despite the Nottinghamshire debacle, more than half the 43 police forces in England and Wales are without the auditing systems necessary to prevent the abuses exposed by the Bedfordshire police. As of April 1998, only four police forces — Greater Manchester, West Midlands, Northumbria and Cleveland — had ceased to pursue secondary detections. It is to be hoped that such initiatives soon spread to all forces, but while the police remain under pressure to fulfil crime targets officers will always be strongly tempted to massage the figures. The Government needs to acknowledge that crude measures and targets for police performance do nothing to enhance public safety. More importantly, it needs to recognise that the police are not the solution to the crime problem and that any meaningful anti-crime strategy must address its root causes.

4 Police Governance

DEMOCRACY AND POLICING

> I am quite convinced that it would be wrong for one man or one government to be in charge directly of the whole police of this country. Our constitution is based on checks and balances, this has kept our liberty through the generations.

This quote is not taken from one of the speeches of Robert Peel when he was establishing professional policing in London in 1829, but rather from a speech by R. A. Butler, the then Home Secretary, at the Summer Conference of the Association of Chief Police Officers in June 1962 (Butler, 1962). What he says is of significance, for he sets out a commitment to an independent police service, free from direct political control, and affirms a principle of independent policing which is considered to be crucial in this country. Nevertheless, this principle although easily stated, has proved to be more difficult to define in practice.

In this chapter we will demonstrate not only that has policing never been entirely free from politics, but also that the way in which police governance has been constructed has meant that in practice everybody involved in the organisation and management is able both to claim credit for successes and disclaim responsibility for failures. The Home Secretary and police authorities could always claim that they were not responsible for failings of policy on the grounds that they related to operational issues. Chief constables could claim that they were unable to achieve their objectives because of lack of proper resources. While these claims are never convincing, they serve to operate as a politically expedient smoke screen which effectively obscures failures of policing policy.

This smoke screen has a long history, and even the Metropolitan Police Act 1829 was a compromise. Peel and his followers had favoured a national police force directly accountable to Parliament. However, Peel faced considerable opposition from influential sections of the community who were worried that a strong national police would become an oppressive arm of government, as had been the case in France. So the Metropolitan Police Act 1829 was only the first step, and policing in Victorian England developed in a piecemeal fashion until the County and Borough Police Act of 1856. The consequence of this was that what developed was a system of essentially local policing, with strong local control. In fact there were cases when the local control was too strong, and Critchley, for example, cites cases where in the 1920s local Watch Committees interfered on an almost daily basis with the Chief Constable's decision-making and with the running of the force (Critchley, 1978).

In general the early years represented something of a struggle between local police authorities and the Home Office, with chief constables being relegated to a subordinate role. Despite many attempts by governments over the years to ensure some form of standardisation over policies and equipment, resulting in a degree of independence being ceded by police authorities to the Home Office, the police service entered the second half of the 20th century in much the same state that it had left the 19th century. By the late 1950s, serious concerns were being raised about the state of policing, and the conduct and accountability of chief constables was in question following a number of disturbing criminal and disciplinary cases. In addition, a series of incidents which today would be regarded as being of relatively minor significance, highlighted the lack of a proper system for recording and investigating complaints against police officers.

ROYAL COMMISSION ON THE POLICE AND THE POLICE ACT 1964

In the face of sustained criticism in the press and frustrations expressed by Members of Parliament at their inability to ask questions of the Home

Secretary about policing outside London, the Government established the Royal Commission on the Police in 1959 (Critchley, 1978). During its deliberations the Royal Commission considered the question of a national police service. In the end it rejected the idea and opted for a system of locally established forces, headed by chief constables, which would be accountable to newly reformed police authorities and to the Home Secretary. This was the so-called tripartite relationship which was intended to bring a balance to the local, national and operational organisation of policing.

The Government accepted the Commission's Report, and in June 1964 the Police Act received Royal Assent. The Police Act 1964 is important because, although it is now over 30 years old and has been superceded by subsequent legislation, it established the basic principles upon which police accountability is founded. The problem which both the Royal Commission and the Government lawyers who drafted the Act had to face was how to express the constitutional arrangement for the organisation and control of the police in a way that established clear lines of accountability, without creating inflexible and proscriptive structures and procedures which would inhibit the effective operation of policing. What the Act did was to introduce a degree of vagueness into the responsibilities of those involved in the tripartite structure. In part this was in recognition of some of the complexities involved in the management of the police in different parts of the country. There remains a suspicion, however, that there was a reluctance to confront some of the difficult constitutional issues that would have been revealed had a more proscriptive approach been adopted.

Under the terms of the 1964 Act the Home Secretary was to be responsible for 'promoting efficiency'. Police authorities had the duty to maintain 'adequate and efficient' police forces, while chief constables were required to exercise 'direction and control' over the force. The Act of course does go on to give specific duties and responsibilities to all parties, but in using vague language it successfully concealed the very real power that it conferred upon the Home Secretary, who was given authority to make regulations governing the overall coordination of policing. As Oliver (1987) observes, it would have been extremely difficult for any chief constable or police authority to act in any way contrary to the wishes of the Home Secretary. In fact, although it was an attempt to establish the constitutional arrangements for the organisation of policing, the ambiguity of terms used in the 1964 Act proved to be contentious almost from the beginning. Unexpectedly, it was the role of chief constables that was to provide the first test. The Royal Commission had considered that the role should be one of independence free from political control. In 1968 the whole question of operational independence was tested in the courts, when Raymond Blackburn commenced an action to force the Metropolitan Police Commissioner to enforce the law rigorously in relation to betting and gaming. Blackburn lost the case; and in his now famous judgment, Lord Denning MR finally established that chief constables were not subject to operational direction by any politician at either local or national level (*R v Commissioner of Police for the Metropolis, ex parte Blackburn* [1968] 2 QB 118).

The Police Act 1964 established police authorities as committees of the local authority made up of two-thirds elected councillors and one-third magistrates. Although it imposed the duty to maintain adequate and efficient police forces, the power of the authorities was severely limited, and in the case of some authorities represented a considerable reduction in influence from what they had previously exercised. One of the few substantial powers that the police authorities retained under the 1964 Act was to appoint chief constables and assistant chief constables, but even there they were restricted to candidates approved by the Home Secretary. There seems little doubt that most police authorities failed to use the powers that they had to any effect and were generally resigned to a role of rubber-stamping the decisions of others. The subordinate position of police authorities was further reinforced in the 1970s and 1980s when serious disputes arose as several of the large urban police authorities attempted to impose a degree of political control on the decisions of their Chief Constables. On those occasions the Chief Constables invariably won support for their operational independence either from the courts, or from the Home Secretary.

It is abundantly clear that by far the most powerful person under the terms of the Police Act 1964 was the Home Secretary, who was empowered to make regulations governing, for example, the size of police forces, police discipline, pay and conditions of service, and police equipment. In addition, it was the Home Secretary who controlled the police grant, which amounted to 51 per cent of the total cost of policing in England and Wales.

In its deliberations the Royal Commission had considered the efficiency of the police service and had recommended that any police force under 500 strong should be regarded as being inefficient. The Police Act 1964 gave the Home Secretary power to order the amalgamation of police forces on grounds of efficiency, and in 1966 Roy Jenkins ordered a reduction in the number of forces from 117 to 49. This necessitated the creation of new combined police authorities in some areas where police forces covering several independent authorities were established, for example Thames Valley and West Mercia. There was a further round of amalgamations in 1974, when the structure of local government in England and Wales was reorganised to create the present 43 police forces — 41 provincial forces, the Metropolitan Police and the City of London Police.

The reorganisation of local authorities in 1974 was an attempt by the then Conservative Government to simplify the structure of local government, creating a system of large and powerful metropolitan counties which had responsibilities for policing. This had the effect of further limiting the influence of police authorities. The local government reforms which brought about the metropolitan counties had effectively created two types of county, each of which was represented in negotiations at national level by its own associations — the Association of Metropolitan Authorities and the Association of County Councils. This meant that police authorities never spoke with one united voice in any forum where policing policy was under discussion. The political landscape in England and Wales during the 1970s and 1980s was a complex one, where the large metropolitan authorities tended to be dominated by Labour councillors while central government from 1979 onwards was Conservative, with a strong law and order agenda. The 1980s can be characterised as a period when the larger metropolitan police authorities attempted to exert political control over (and to an extent to wrest operational control from) Chief Constables, in the face of a central Government increasingly concerned to improve the financial accountability of the police service and to limit the power of the local authorities across a whole range of activities, including policing.

Disputes between on the one side the Chief Constables and the Home Office, and on the otherside powerful police authorities, especially following the 1981 inner-city disturbances and the miners' dispute of 1984/85, saw attempts by police authorities to exert control defeated in the courts and by the exercise of regulatory power by the Home Office. By the end of the 1980s the battle for political control had been lost, but the Home Secretary had effectively begun to alter the balance and to make the police financially accountable.

SOCIAL CHANGES

What neither the Royal Commission nor those who drafted the Police Act 1964 could have foreseen were the tremendous social changes which were to take place during the 1970s and 1980s, which fundamentally altered the way in which the police service was to operate.

The first of these changes was the beginning of a series of terrorist campaigns, initially in the form of the Irish Republican Campaign, which spread to England and Wales in the 1970s following the outbreak of the troubles in Northern Ireland in 1969. However, there was also international terrorism, with aircraft hi-jacking and bombings linked to political causes elsewhere in the world.

The second was the growth of organised serious crime which had a national rather than a local character. While it is still true that most crime is committed within a four-mile radius of the offender's home, it became clear during the 1970s that improved road communications throughout the country meant that a growing number of serious professional criminals could travel relatively easily, committing crimes well away from their home towns. During this time more sophisticated investigative techniques, including the use of information technology, enabled detectives to link crimes which would previously have been regarded as purely local events. The eventual introduction of the computerised Home Office Major Enquiry system has been an invaluable tool to police officers investigating increasingly complex criminal activities around the country.

The third change was the emergence of international crime, particularly drug trafficking and the laundering of money associated with the drug trade.

The fourth was the growth in the 1980s of violence and disorder on a scale which had not been seen for many years. Individual police forces found themselves unable to deal with some of the most severe outbreaks and had to rely on mutual aid from other forces.

The result of all of these changes was a realisation of the need for a degree of standardisation of equipment and practices across police forces, which could be achieved only by central coordination. The need to exchange information, for example, required all forces to share a common database — the Police National Computer. Effective mutual aid required compatible radio equipment, and increasingly sophisticated (often international) criminal investigations required that equipment to be secured from unauthorised access. Increasingly, decisions about policing were being taken at central rather than at local level.

NEW PUBLIC MANAGEMENT

One of the key objectives of the Conservative Government which came to power in 1979 was to make local government more efficient and accountable, and much of its early policy was intended to achieve that objective. Although the police found themselves in a highly privileged position in relation to the provision of resources, they were still expected to exercise prudence in the manner in which those resources were being used. From 1983 onwards, the Government tightened its control on the way in which the police were managed, and by the 1990s it was clearly determined that the service would adopt all of the rigour of New Public Management which had earlier been enforced in the National Health Service and education.

Immediately after its election victory in 1992, the Government began to consider its strategy for dealing with the problem of the police. There was serious dissatisfaction among senior ministers that, despite their generosity to the service since 1979, crime had continued to rise and detections had continued to fall. There was disillusionment with the criminal justice system as a whole, but the police bore the brunt of the criticism. Part of the blame for police failures was also laid at the door of the police authorities, particularly those in the metropolitan counties which the Government considered had been obstructive during the whole of the 1980s and which by 1992 were overwhelmingly dominated by politicians opposed to Government policies. The Home Secretary ordered an inquiry into police responsibility and rewards, the Sheehy Inquiry, and a report into police core and ancillary tasks, the Posen report. In addition, a White Paper on police reform was published, which formed the basis of the Police and Magistrates' Courts Bill. The Bill was introduced into the House of Lords and was subject to a great deal of critical debate and amendment. Had it been enacted in its original form, it would have had the effect of centralising all responsibility for policing under the Home Secretary and reducing the role of the police authority to that of a sinecure. As it transpired, amendments forced upon the Government meant that the resulting Police and Magistrates' Courts Act 1994 was greatly modified from its original intent. The Act did not repeal the Police Act 1964 but it amended it and extended it in a number of important respects.

POLICE AND MAGISTRATES' COURTS ACT 1994

The Police and Magistrates' Courts Act 1994 has been described as being both a centralising and a de-centralising piece of legislation. It gave the Home Secretary the power to set key policing objectives, and ultimately control over the total amount of money available to finance each police force. It was de-centralising because it gave Chief Constables and police authorities much greater flexibility than previously as to how the money was spent. In a very real sense it extended the process which, under the influence of the Audit Commission and HM's Inspectorate of Constabulary, had been underway for several years, whereby responsibility for decisions and financial management was devolved to operational commanders at local level. At the same time it established a mechanism which allowed the publication of league tables, thus allowing results to be compared across a range of centrally determined performance indicators.

The key changes to police governance under the Police and Magistrates' Courts Act 1994 affected each of the constituents of the tripartite relationship. The chief constable was responsible for the day-to-day management of the force and retained operational independence, and police authorities were considerably restructured under the Act. The 1964 legislation specified the proportions of councillors and magistrates in the police authority but made no stipulation as to size. The creation of metropolitan counties in 1974 had resulted in a number of very large police authorities, and in an attempt to ensure proper political representation some had become unwieldy. The Police and Magistrates' Courts Act 1994 established police authorities as free-standing bodies, as opposed to being committees of the local authority, and stipulated their size as well as their composition. Under the terms of the 1994 Act, police authorities normally comprised 17 members, although the Home Secretary had the power to approve an increase in the size to an odd number greater than 17. The normal composition was nine elected councillors, five independent members and three magistrates. The five independent members were appointed from a shortlist approved by the Home Secretary, and the chair of the authority was elected from within the membership. The duty of the police authority was to 'secure the maintenance of a efficient and effective police force for its area' (Police and Criminal Evidence Act 1984, s. 106).

The greatest change in the new legislation concerned the role of the Home Secretary. Under the 1964 Act, the Home Secretary exercised considerable control over the size and composition of police forces. The Home Secretary approved the overall size of the force and controlled capital expenditure. That power was devolved in 1994 to chief constables and police authorities, but the Home Secretary now controlled the overall expenditure on each force by means of the cash limited police grant. In other key respects the power of the Home Secretary was increased by virtue of the authority to set key policing objectives and performance targets against which all police forces would be judged. Thus the means by which policing policy is now determined is that each year the Home Secretary will announce his key performance objectives and performance targets. Each chief constable is then required to produce a draft policing plan, which must take into account the needs of the local area and the Home Secretary's objectives. The police authority then uses the draft plan as a blueprint, and after consultation with the community produces the annual costed policing plan which forms the basis for the police budget for that year.

ADVISORY AND OTHER ORGANISATIONS

Her Majesty's Inspectorate of Constabulary

In performing the above duties the Home Secretary must be satisfied that each police force is efficient and effective. The organisation which is charged with responsibility for ensuring efficiency is HM's Inspectorate of Constabulary.

Her Majesty's Inspectorate of Constabulary was first established in 1856, when, under the County and Borough Police Act, the Government required all local authorities to establish police forces. The Act authorised the Home Secretary to make available a 25 per cent grant towards the cost of establishing and running the force. The Inspectorate was set up to ensure that the newly-formed forces were efficient. Although very active in the 19th and early 20th centuries, by the 1960s the Inspectorate had become little more than a sinecure for retired senior Chief Constables.

Constitutionally the Inspectorate was established as a body independent both of the police service and the Home Office, and was charged with responsibility to advise and assist both. The Police Act 1964 reinforced its role in securing efficiency and established the office of Chief Inspector of Constabulary, specifically to provide advice to the Home Secretary on policing matters. The Inspectorate had the duty to inspect forces on an annual basis and was required to satisfy itself that each force was efficient. If satisfied, it issued a certificate of efficiency, and it was only once that certificate had been issued that the Home Secretary authorised the payment of the police support grant.

In the 1980s the role of the Inspectorate began to be enhanced. Following the disturbances of 1981, a number of the larger police authorities attempted to prevent chief constables from obtaining specialised equipment to enable them to deal effectively with further outbreaks of disorder. The chief constables appealed to the Home Secretary who set up a central store of equipment which could be made available with the approval of the Inspectorate. During the mid-1980s, in a drive to secure greater efficiency from the police service, the Home Office embarked upon a policy of encouraging chief constables to employ civilians to perform roles which did not require specific police powers, and thus release police officers for operational duties. In order to ensure that this policy was implemented, the Inspectorate was required to include civilianisation on its agenda when conducting inspections, and increases to police force establishments were made conditional upon the achievement of an appropriate level of civilian support staff. By 1989 the Inspectorate was further boosted by the appointment by a number of young ex-chief constables who were considered to be in their prime, and thus were likely to move on to other senior posts. In 1990, it was decided that Inspectorate reports which had previously been private documents circulated only to the Home Secretary, chief constable and police authority were to be published, thus opening up every police force to public scrutiny.

The Police and Magistrates' Courts Act 1994 extended the role of the Inspectorate still further by asking it to consider questions of effectiveness, but it did not increase the power of the Inspectorate. Thus, Her Majesty's Inspectorate of Constabulary now acts as an advisory body seeking to achieve improvements in policing by the dissemination of best practice. Each police force is required to undergo inspection when it is subjected to the scrutiny of an experienced team from one of the Inspectorate's regional offices. The programme and focus for inspections is determined annually at a meeting of all the inspectors, chaired by the chief inspector. One of the ways in which they have increased their influence over the service is by highlighting particular areas of policy or practice which will be subjected to scrutiny. In this way they can ensure that policy set out in Home Office circulars is being followed by police forces.

Of late the Inspectorate has further diversified and extended its activities by undertaking a number of what are termed 'thematic' inspections. These inspections relate not to individual police forces, but to the way in which the police service as a whole is responding to a particular issue or area of responsibility. Examples of thematic inspections which have been particularly influential in recent years include 'Equal Opportunities' and 'Value for Money'.

The Audit Commission

Without doubt, the decision in 1990 to publish inspection reports has had a considerable influence on the way in which police forces are run, but there is one further way in which the Inspectorate has been able to bring about greater coordination of policing. That is through the relationship it has established with the Audit Commission.

The Audit Commission was established under the Local Government Finance Act 1982 as a independent, self-financing body with responsibility to examine the provision of all local authority services, and to make recommendations to secure improvements in economy, efficiency and effectiveness. It published the first of a series of highly influential reports on the police service in 1988, and has since proved a major influence in establishing innovative practices into operational policing.

The police service has been highly responsive to the recommendations of the Audit Commission, and is generally regarded to have had the most positive response of any organisation in the public sector. This can be attributed to a number of factors. The first reports of the Audit Commission, for example, dealt with issues which were peripheral to operational policing and were concerned with vehicle police management, the organisation of scenes of crime services, etc. The Audit Commission recommended changes which were regarded as beneficial and which were valued by the service, which was at the time struggling to demonstrate to the Government that it was taking the need for efficiency seriously. Subsequent papers continued in this way and recommended changes to existing practice which were based on thoughtful, well-conducted research. Even if at times the Commission's reports were critical of some police management practices, its recommendations were attractive to the service because they offered tangible results, at a time when policing was subject to increasing scrutiny from a Government bent on reform.

In recent years the Audit Commission has been remarkably successful in encouraging change in police policy in a number of significant areas. For example, Audit Commission reports have resulted in the devolution of command and managerial responsibility to local operational commanders; in developing a more structured and targeted approach to uniform patrol duties; and in developing an approach to crime detection which focuses on the criminal rather than the crime — an approach known as 'intelligence led policing'. Yet the Audit Commission, like the Inspectorate of Constabulary, has no formal power and can only make observations and recommendations.

Operation of the Inspectorate and the Commission

It is instructive to examine how the two organisations operate. Both organisations are established in law with specific functions with respect to the police (exclusively, in the case of the Inspectorate, and as part of a comprehensive remit to review general authority services in the case of the Audit Commission). Both have a consultancy role to advise and promote best practice in addition to their inspection functions. Because the Inspectorate is composed mainly of ex-Chief Constables, assisted by a number of staff officers drawn from the senior ranks of the service, its expertise and knowledge is assumed and respected. The Audit Commission, on the other hand, compiles its reports from empirically generated data and produces recommendations based on argument supported by evidence. When they both agree on the desirability of a particular course of action, it is difficult for any but the strongest of Chief Constables to dissent. But in any event, the history of the police service has been one of increasing centralisation, with real effective power being ceded to the Home Office. Policing is now a much more corporate activity, driven to achieve results and influenced by theory and the evaluation of policies and strategies more than at any time in its past. In fact the police service has seen more change since 1964 than in all of its previous history.

Police Federation, Superintendents Association and the Association of Chief Police Officers

So far we have described something of the duties of those official bodies charged with responsibility for policing, but they tell us little of the processes which are involved in developing policy and ensuring that it is put into place. Neither do they tell us anything about the negotiating processes which have a considerable influence on the development of police policy. Clearly, in any organisation the employees have a considerable influence on the way in which policies are implemented, but in the case of the police service they have become increasingly influential in recent years not only in implementing policy, but also in developing policy initiatives.

Police officers are forbidden by law to be members of a trade union, or to take any active part in politics. They do, however, have a right to be represented at both national and local level in discussions regarding pay and conditions of service. In this respect police officers are represented by one of three staff associations, membership of which is determined by the rank which they hold. Civilian support staff are not bound by the same statutory restrictions which affect police officers and are free to be members of established trade unions.

The majority of police officers holding the ranks from constable to chief inspector are represented by the Police Federation. The Superintendents Association represents officers holding the rank of superintendent, while the Association of Chief Police Officers (ACPO) represents chief constables and assistant chief constables. Although they have no formal role in policy making, the trend in recent years has been for the Home Office to involve all of the staff associations in discussions at all stages of the process. While their role in these circumstances is limited and they have no power of veto, they have become increasingly influential. There is little doubt, for example, that it was the sustained campaign by the Police Federation during the late 1970s (for improved pay and conditions for junior police officers) which raised the profile of the law and order debate to the extent that it became an important focus during the General Election campaign of 1979. More recently, the Police Federation has been at the forefront of campaigns for increased police powers to deal with crime and social problems. But the role of the Police Federation has been more akin to that of a pressure group than of a organisation with direct access to government and with the ability to shape policy in a very direct way. The role of ACPO, on the other hand, has been much more direct and it has become an important contributor to the development of new policing practices. In contrast, the trade unions which represent civilian employees have had very little effect on the development of policing policy, despite the fact that they have the potential to represent a workforce of some 40,000 people. The recent history of trade unionism in England and Wales is, of course, one of declining membership and influence, and police civilians have never been strongly unionised and remain largely unrepresented in discussions over changes in policing policy. The Superintendents Association is the least influential of the three staff associations, although even it in recent years has raised its profile to become a significant body in discussing legislative and policy change.

By far the most influential organisation is ACPO which remains a staff association established to represent the interests of its members. However, in recent years it has become an important organisation for the coordination and implementation of policing policy nationally. It is consulted by Government on proposals for new legislation, and while its opinion is not always taken into account, it certainly has the opportunity to present the police's point of view. When the Home Office needs to inform the service about changes in legislation policy or procedure, it does so by means of Home Office circulars. These circulars have no statutory force and their status is advisory rather than compulsory. However, ACPO is invariably involved in the early stages of drafting circulars, and as a consequence they have generally been agreed before they are published. In the rare circumstances where a chief constable would wish to ignore a Home Officer circular, he or she would almost certainly incur the displeasure of his or her colleagues and would invariably be subject to criticism from the Inspectorate of Constabulary. In addition, ACPO constitutes a very powerful pressure group, in much the same way as the Police Federation, which lobbies for changes in policy or increases in police powers.

There is one way in which ACPO has become even more significant in recent years. It acts as a coordinating body which determines how policing policy will be implemented nationally. To illustrate this point, let us consider a number of examples. It used to be the case that people were encouraged to fit burglar alarms to commercial premises, and if an alarm was activated the police would attend. It soon became clear that the majority of alarms were activated due to faults in the system or faults in the way in which the alarm had been set. As the number of burglar alarm installations increased, so did the demands on the police. Inevitably police were attending a huge number of false alarms, which tied up resources at a time when demands on the service were increasing. The response of ACPO was to establish a national policy which set out the police's conditions for responding to burglar alarms. This policy required the alarm to be installed by a reputable company, and it stipulated that if there were three successive fault calls the police response would be withdrawn until the fault was satisfactorily rectified. More recent examples have been highlighted by a number of national newspapers, which have revealed that ACPO has determined that police forces will adopt a national policy with respect to the enforcement of speed limits. The policy became subject to debate because it effectively raised speed limits by setting a level of speed which would need to be achieved before the police would prosecute. In fact there was nothing particularly new in this — ACPO had agreed prosecution guidelines for years — but it has highlighted the fact that chief constables are using their operational independence to determine policies which are justifiable in terms of the police's use of resources, but which have implications for the way in which legislation is interpreted. There is in fact considerable logic in the police service agreeing policies about how to enforce the law, but the problem is that ACPO is effectively a non-accountable body. It makes its policies behind closed doors and without public scrutiny.

A final important role of ACPO is its articulation of policing policy to the Government and the public alike. Specific aspects of policing will require an ACPO committee to consider the position of the service, and each committee will have a representative who will be the police spokesperson on its area of interest. The service has for a number of years been moving away from 'local solutions to local problems' to a situation where there is a nationally agreed response for any identified situation. It is, of course, true that ACPO has no power to compel its members to abide by particular decisions and there are numerous examples of where this does not happen. Nevertheless, we are at a point in our history where there is far more coordination of policing that at any time previously.

CLOSE TO THE PUBLIC — POLICING BY CONSENT?

In all of this, it is important that the practice of policing should be informed at every level by the public. After all, we do pride ourselves in Britain that we 'police by consent'. Yet in his 1981 Report on the Brixton disorders, Lord Scarman was very critical of the police for having lost contact with the public. He recommended that all forces should be required to establish bodies through which effective consultation and discussion could take place, and where policing priorities could be established. A number of police forces immediately took up the recommendation without waiting for a Government response, but the Police and Criminal Evidence Act 1984 established a requirement for all police authorities to establish local police consultative committees (Home Office, 1991). It became clear almost immediately that the arrangements for consultation were not working satisfactorily. Community representatives tended to be self-appointed interest groups with no mandate to speak on behalf of their communities. Ethnic minorities, the young, the unemployed and minority groups were rarely represented, and all too often consultative committees became venues at which senior police commanders explained the problems that the local police faced and took little (if any) notice of points raised at the meeting. As one police commander we interviewed recently commented:

> when I go to my consultative committee I should be the only one white person there, I police an area which is predominately made up of people of Asian or Afro Caribbean origin. Yet I hardly ever see representatives from those communities and there is never anyone under the age of 35 present at the meetings.

Even if the consultative committees were working effectively, it is doubtful if they would ever provide a satisfactory forum for discussion about policing policy. If we assume that on average each police force has 11 command units (and that is an over-estimation), and each has an effective committee of (say) 35 members, as there are 43 police forces in England and Wales this means that 16,500 people would be involved out of a total population of around 60 million in England and Wales. There are very few who would regard that as effective communication and consultation.

Of course, the Police and Magistrates' Courts Act 1994 requires the police authority to consult on the contents of the annual policing plan.

So we could be forgiven if we were to suppose that at that point at least there would be some effective dialogue. Unfortunately that is not the case, because the Act envisages that the consultation will be undertaken using the facilities established under the Police and Criminal Evidence Act 1984. It would seem, therefore, that the public have no effective voice in determining policing policy. The Home Secretary will claim that he listens to public opinion when formulating his key policing objectives, and that the public always have an opportunity to express their views at the time of an election. The chief constables will say that the local commanders are in daily contact with their committees and that local policing is sensitive to local needs. So it may be, but it has to be remembered that the performance of each basic command unit is judged against criteria determined first and foremost in response to nationally set objectives rather than to local concerns. Police authorities are in an even more difficult position, their contact with community concerns is mediated through the elected members and the flawed mechanism of the consultative committee.

In recognition of these problems, the police service has in recent years taken to using public opinion surveys in order to gauge the community's reaction to the manner in which it is being policed. Although the results of such surveys are often positive, they do also reveal some rather disturbing information. Some communities, for example, are much less satisfied than others about the quality of the policing that they experience, and they are often critical of police performance.

There is one other method by which the police can assess information about the public reaction to the service, and that is the British Crime Survey (BCS). This is not a mechanism for consultation but is a survey set up by the Home Office in 1982 which has been conducted every two years since to provide a picture of the experience of crime amongst the general public. The reason for establishing the BCS was the acknowledgement that official crime statistics did not provide an accurate picture of crime in Britain, because for a variety of reasons many crimes did not come to the notice of the police. The BCS asks a number of questions about the respondents' experience of crime, together with their reasons for reporting or not reporting an incident to the police. It consistently reveals a level of crime which is higher than that recorded in official statistics, and the various reasons why people do not report crime to the police. These range from the fact that the crime is too trivial to the fact that there is no chance of anyone being caught; from the belief that the police are too busy to the belief that the police are not interested. Although it is not a consultative mechanism, it should give the police service some pause for thought.

In the 1998 BCS, people were asked about their contact with the police and their assessment of police performance. Similarly victims who had reported crimes to the police were also asked about the service they received. The results of this research would seem to suggest that the majority of the public (81 per cent) felt that the police in their area did a good job. However, some groups tended to have a more favourable view towards their local police than others. Those with particularly favourable views were those: (i) aged 60 or over; (ii) in households with annual incomes over £30,000; and (iii) living in rural areas. Thus, those who tended to be more critical of the police were typically between the ages of 16 and 29, earning less than £10,000 per annum and living within inner cities (Yeo and Budd, 2000). Indeed, a fifth of adults interviewed recalled being 'really annoyed' by the behaviour of a police officer — largely because the police had been rude or unfriendly, had behaved unreasonably or had failed to do anything.

THE CRIME AND DISORDER ACT 1998

The Police and Magistrates' Courts Act 1994 sets out the principles which govern the accountability and management of policing in England and Wales, and as we have indicated, it has continued a trend towards the centralisation of power over policing to the office of the Home Secretary. However the position with regard to the police has been further complicated by a more recent piece of legislation — the Crime and Disorder Act 1998.

The 1998 Act is principally a measure which establishes a number of initiatives intended to reduce youth crime and to deal with crime and anti-social behaviour. It is of particular relevance to our discussion because it removes the prime responsibility for crime prevention from the police and places it instead with the local authority. In this respect it follows the recommendations of the Morgan Report (1991). This was commissioned by the last Conservative Government, but some of its recommendations were largely shelved during the lifetime of that Government, primarily because of the Administration's mistrust of local government. The Morgan Report recognised that crime prevention was a community problem which involved the police, but which was far too wide for the police alone to be able to deal with effectively. The Labour Government, in 1997, accepted the recommendations of the Morgan Report and, under the Crime and Disorder Act 1998, placed a statutory duty on local authorities to coordinate the activities of all statutory and voluntary agencies to produce an audit of crime and disorder problems and action plans intended to deal with them.

There are two real and very significant problems with part of the Act. First, the local authorities to which it refers are not the same as police authorities, and neither do they represent the same area. Local authority boundaries, for the purposes of the Crime and Disorder Act 1998, are not coterminous with police force boundaries but relate more closely to basic command units (BCUs) or operational command units (OCUs). This creates something of a dilemma, because the policing plan relates to the force area and to nationally prescribed policing objectives, whereas the crime and disorder plan relates specifically to local problems. The second problem involves finance. All of the agencies involved have priorities assessed on the basis of national targets or plans, and while, policing has already been discussed, other agencies face similar problems. Health, for example, will be focused on national priorities and targets, while education has to deal with the demands of the national curriculum. Nowhere in the Crime and Disorder Act 1998 is there any indication of how the various schemes are to be financed. It is true that the Government has made some additional money available through, for example, the Crime Fighting Fund, but that is necessarily limited and will only supplement local provision. It is also inevitable that budgets that are calculated on the basis of national priorities will not be spent on local targets, where performance will be judged against the key national priorities.

There is one further problem with the Crime and Disorder Act 1998, which again relates to consultation. Local authorities are required to consult widely about problems and plans, and one of the vehicles envisaged for that consultation is the flawed provision of local consultative committees.

None of this is necessarily fatal and there are indeed examples of local partnerships producing encouraging results. It is however too early to form a clear picture of the effects of the 1998 Act on operational policing — and we should perhaps take the optimistic view that it will provide a real opportunity for the development of policing policy which is generally rooted in local priorities — however, previous experience does not provide much ground for optimism.

CONCLUSION

There has always been a tension between local and national priorities, and the recent past has seen an inexorable drift towards a police service driven by national priorities determined by the Home Office. Chief constables have emerged as increasingly influential, but only within the context of an agenda set by the Home Secretary. In the dying years of the last Conservative Government, proposals were discussed for a further round of amalgamations which could potentially reduce the number of police forces from the present 43 to around 20. Inevitably that would lead to further centralisation and a loss of local identity.

The police service is now more financially accountable than at any time in history, and policing policy is determined at national rather than local level. Crime rates continue to increase, as does the fear of crime, while at the same time public confidence in the police is falling. Much of the rhetoric which surrounds the police service today revolves around the notion of local accountability and responding to local concerns and problems, yet the reality is different, and we would argue that the police service in England and Wales is effectively unaccountable. The Home Secretary can set national targets, but the responsibility to meet those targets is in the hands of chief constables and police authorities over whom he has no direct operational control. Chief constables can always maintain that they lack sufficient resources to meet all of the priorities that are identified, while the police authorities have little real authority and there is no effective mechanism to hold them accountable.

5 Malpractice

INTRODUCTION

Ask a police officer if his profession is properly accountable and the chances are that he will say it is the most closely regulated of all public institutions. He may reel off a list of bodies to which the police are accountable — HM Inspectorate of Constabulary, the courts, the Crown Prosecution Service, the Police Complaints Authority, community liaison panels, Neighbourhood Watch groups and victim support schemes. Furthermore, he might add, the police are bound by a disciplinary code governed by an Act of Parliament, and chief constables are accountable to their police authorities and ultimately to the Home Secretary. The chances are that he will lament that this amounts to over-regulation which makes it impossible for officers to do their job properly.

Ask the same question of someone who has a grievance against the police and the answer will likely be very different. That person will probably claim that the police are a law unto themselves and that the various bodies entrusted with holding them to account are at best paper tigers, or at worst actively collude in the covering up of malpractice.

So where does the truth lie? We have suggested that the police are effectively unaccountable and in this chapter we examine the problems of police wrongdoing. Malpractice can take many forms, from the relatively trivial through to outright criminal corruption, and policing can become corrupted without corrupt policemen. Furthermore, a substantial grey area exists between legitimate investigative techniques and outright malpractice and corruption. Malpractice and corruption can be, of course, features of any profession, but the fact that the police are entrusted by the public with upholding the law means that their misdemeanours are uniquely corrosive of public confidence. In Chapter 3 we examined the way in which some police forces manipulated crime figures, but such abuses are not generally regarded as being corrupt *per se*.

ONE BAD APPLE?

The image of police corruption most often served up by our popular culture, is of a Scotland Yard detective, dressed in trilby and raincoat, taking a back-hander from a sharp-suited gang leader in a 1960s Soho nightclub. It is an image legitimised in large measure by Sir Robert Mark, who, having been appointed Commissioner of the Metropolitan Police in 1972, made the astonishing declaration that his Criminal Investigation Department was 'the most routinely corrupt organisation in London'. Despite the efforts of Mark and other chief constables to purge the police of corruption, some career criminals maintain that it has always remained rife. The average police officer, on the other hand, will generally say that the problem extends only to the occasional 'bad apple'.

Corruption by its very nature tends to be covert, which makes it impossible to evaluate the scale of the problem properly. All that is certain is that is has not gone away. In February 1997, for example, the directors-general of the country's two elite national police bodies, the National Crime Squad (NCS) and the National Criminal Intelligence Service (NCIS), announced a major corruption inquiry involving the suspension of some of their officers. An outside force was invited in to investigate a number of claims, including a corrupt relationship with an important police informant. The NCS was established in 1998 as an elite team of detectives whose work was meant to compliment the intelligence-gathering activities of NCIS (*Guardian*, 27 February 1999).

In 1994, the Metropolitan Police launched a major anti-corruption drive to be handled by the force's complaints investigation branch (CIB3). Four years later the force's then Commissioner, Sir Paul Condon, announced a further initiative which he promised would be the most comprehensive anti-corruption strategy ever devised by a police force (*Guardian*, 12 December 1998). By February 1999, 57 officers had been suspended and 35 charges brought as a result of the initiative. Elsewhere, nearly half of the 43 police forces in England and Wales had officers facing corruption or dishonesty allegations. A total of more than 100 officers from 19 forces were suspended or charged over allegations relating to the misuse of police information, drug offences or perverting the course of justice (*Guardian*, 27 February 1999).

In 1999, no less a figure than the head of CIB3, David Wood, announced that he was 'astonished' by some of the corrupt practices he had uncovered. Placed in charge of the unit's team of 200 officers, he found that some officers had put the lives of undercover officers at risk by 'feeding back intelligence' of their identities to the criminals who were being monitored. Wood said: 'What astonishes me is that police officers are quite prepared to lapse into these contracts with organised crime (with the result that) cases they know their colleagues have taken months to put together, and cost millions of pounds, are being undermined.' CIB3 discovered that for between £5,000 and £7,000, crooked officers would provide a false statement. There was an 'ongoing rate' of £50,000 to £60,000 for undermining a court case, and up to £100,000 had been paid to undermine a major trial. All such payments were made in cash and could not be traced. These discoveries prompted Scotland Yard to consider introducing rigorous vetting procedures on around 2,000 detectives working in the most security-sensitive posts. Such vetting would examine unauthorised criminal contacts and personal problems of the kind that might make them vulnerable to bribery and blackmail (*Independent*, 24 May 1999).

Six years on from its launch, the anti-corruption drive appeared to have made slow progress. By March 2000, there had been only seven prosecutions for major corruption. The Crown Prosecution Service had decided not to proceed against 80 officers, and of the 70 officers by then suspended as a result of CIB3's investigations, more than two-thirds had not been charged. More seriously, CIB3 was itself the subject of three major inquiries concerning its methods of investigation, which were shown to have included entrapment and inducements to super-grasses. The unit also came under fire for failing to disclose vital documents to the defence in court cases. Defence solicitors complained that such abuses marked a return to the discredited police methods of the 1960s and 1970s, which resulted in many miscarriages of justice (these abuses are discussed later in this chapter) (*Guardian*, 4 March 2000).

The behaviour of some police officers is clearly corrupt and clearly criminal, but in other cases such rigid distinctions are elusive. This point was underlined in a 1999 study by HM Inspectorate of Constabulary, entitled *Police Integrity — Security and Maintaining Public Confidence.* The report, which Home Secretary Jack Straw admitted made 'uncomfortable reading', found that officers in different forces were told that they could accept gifts, ranging from a £100 watch to a brace of pheasants. In some forces they were allowed cheap holidays, cut-price entrance to the cinemas and night clubs, and free travel on public transport. Blaming poor management and leadership, the report stated: 'Staff have never been told what practices are unacceptable. It is clearly insufficient to assume common sense will prevail.' The report was clear that an example had to be set from the top, and observed: 'Some chief officers talk of zero tolerance, but this is viewed with some cynicism by their junior officers who feel the acceptance by senior officers of free business lunches and drinking alcohol whilst on duty at public functions is a double standard.' (*Guardian*, 11 June 1999).

'NOBLE-CAUSE CORRUPTION'

Just as most police officers would make a distinction between outright criminal corruption and the type of breaches outlined in the HM Inspectorate of Constabulary report, they would also generally distinguish between corruption that is practised for the purely personal ends and that which is practised for the laudable end of law enforcement. The latter, most commonly, consists in rule-bending with the aim of securing a conviction that might otherwise not have occurred. For this reason it is known as 'noble-cause corruption'.

As with outright criminal corruption, the extent of noble-cause corruption is impossible to measure, but whereas outright corruption is anathema to the majority of officers, noble-cause corruption tends to be more accepted because obtaining convictions, or 'getting results' as it is known, is central to their occupational culture (see Chapter 7). 'Investigating officers become convinced that someone is guilty, but they know they've not got enough evidence to stand the case up in court', says a former detective interviewed for this book, 'there's an unwritten code that it's OK to break the rules in these circumstances. Usually only a few of the officers on the case are involved and those who stumble across it will just turn a blind eye.' (Interview, August 1999).

As well as being a matter of personal and professional pride for most officers, obtaining convictions is also their passport to promotion and an improved salary. As we explained in Chapter 3, the introduction of police performance targets and league tables in the 1990s increased the pressure to get results. Unfortunately, getting results and uncovering the truth about a crime do not always amount to the same thing. Although most successful prosecutions result in the right people being convicted, innocent people are sometimes ensnared. Noble-cause corruption is often at the core of such cases. There are any number of ways in which the police can bend the rules of investigation in their own favour — far too many, indeed, to explore in this chapter. It is nevertheless worth mentioning two of the most common, because, as we will describe below, there is a danger that legislative changes introduced by the last Conservative Government, with the support of the Labour Opposition, may promote such abuses.

The failure to investigate and disclose evidence

As one academic has put it, 'If any one factor in investigative practice had to be nominated as most responsible for leading to miscarriages [of justice], it would have to be the tendency for investigators to commit themselves to belief in a suspect's guilt in a way which blinds them to other possibilities' (Dixon, 1999). In the course of an investigation, evidence may emerge which appears to provide the suspect with an alibi, or indicating that others may have in fact committed the crime. A hallmark of many of the miscarriage of justice cases that came to light in the past decade is the fact that much of the evidence which eventually proved critical in overturning the convictions was lying in police files but had never been disclosed to the defence prior to the original trial.

No doubt, in such cases the officers who led the original investigation convinced themselves that this exculpatory evidence was unreliable, or plain mistaken. There have, however, been cases where it is difficult to see how this justification could be sustained. Take, for example, the conviction of Stefan Kisko, who was jailed for life in 1976 for the murder of schoolgirl Lesley Molseed. The conviction rested on a confession which the emotionally immature Kisko signed under duress and later retracted. Incredibly, the police were in possession of semen tests which showed he could not possibly have been the killer, but never handed these to the defence (Wilson, 1999).

In the wake of the over-turning of the conviction of Judith Ward, who was wrongly convicted in 1974 for two IRA bombings, the Court of Appeal ruled that the Crown Prosecution Service should be duty bound to hand over all case material to the defence. In Ward's case, as in Kisko's, the prosecution had withheld evidence which might well have led to her acquittal at the original trial.

The police complained that the ruling would benefit unscrupulous defendants, because the so-called unused material often contained false leads to other potential suspects. In the hands of a skilful defence barrister, such red herrings might result in an acquittal. They also complained that copying vast quantities of unused material would be costly and time-consuming. Conservative Home Secretary Michael Howard agreed and steered through Parliament the Criminal Procedure and Investigations Act 1996. The Act, which applies to the prosecution of all crimes committed after 1 April 1997, obliges a defendant to make a statement which is provided to the prosecution. On the basis of this, the prosecution will decide what evidence in its possession is relevant to the defence case, and it is only that evidence that it is obliged to hand over. The job of judging which evidence is relevant falls not to a Crown Prosecution Service solicitor, but to police disclosure officers, who in some parts of the country are detective constables who will inevitably have limited experience or understanding of how defence barristers prepare their case. To make matters worse, some disclosure officers have privately voiced concern that investigating officers deliberately fail to tell them about all the evidence in a case.

The 1996 Act received an almost universally hostile reception from criminal law specialists. The authors of the main academic guide (Leng and Taylor, 1996) to the legislation said that the Act had been passed by an 'ambush' of Parliament, and added that time constraints meant that 'large sections of the Bill were hardly considered at all'. Surveys by both the Law Society and the Bar Council among their respective member-ship found major problems with the way the Act was being applied. The leader of the Law Society survey, Roger Ede, described the situation as 'pretty horrifying', while Anthony Heaton-Armstrong of the Bar Council said that the police and Crown Prosecution Service were not telling the defence about 'information which obviously seriously undermines the prosecution case or strengthens the defence, in circumstances that the Act anticipates that they would do' (*Guardian*, 4 May 1999). Typically, the prosecution would not disclose statements by one of their witnesses which contained details that were at variance with a subsequent statement that was being relied upon to bring the prosecution. Cross-examining prosecution witnesses on the discrepancies in their statements is one of the main tactics open to defence barristers. The most telling criticism of the 1996 Act came from none other than the head of the Crown Prosecution Service, Director of Public Prosecutions, David Calvert-Smith QC, who publicly voiced his concern that the Act would lead to more miscarriages of justice.

False confessions and the right to silence

Obtaining confessions is one of the most cost-effective ways of clearing a crime, as it saves time and potentially expensive investigation. Under criminal law, once a person becomes a suspect he or she must be informed of that fact and cautioned that anything he or she tells the police from that point onwards may be used as evidence against him or her in court. The subsequent police interviews with the suspect are therefore usually critical. Over the years the police devised a number of interview strategies to obtain convictions. In extreme cases, such as that of the so-called Birmingham Six (the six men who were wrongly convicted of the 1974 Birmingham pub bombings), they would fabricate confessions (Rose, 1997). In other cases the police were simply economical in what they recorded in the notes of the interview. More often they would bring a variety of tried and tested techniques to bear on the interrogation — some subtle, some less so. These ranged from oppressive questioning and outright bullying, to gentle persuasion. If two suspects were questioned for the same crime, they might be told separately that the other had confessed and that it was in each of their interests to admit their role but claim that the other was the main instigator.

Such abuses were one of the factors that prompted the introduction of the Police and Criminal Evidence Act 1984 (PACE). Disliked by detectives, the Act introduced a raft of new procedural requirements to govern the conduct of interviews and enhance the rights of suspects. Among the most important innovations was the requirement that all formal interviews be contemporaneously recorded, which almost

always meant that they were tape-recorded, and that suspects were
required to verify the accuracy of the record. Confessions deemed to
have been obtained by oppressive methods, or other conduct likely to
render them unreliable, were excluded as evidence in any subsequent
prosecution. The Act also required a custody officer, independent of the
investigation, to be assigned to ensure the welfare of the suspect and
adherence to the rules.

The high-profile miscarriages of justice that came to light in the late
1980s and early 1990s were put down to pre-PACE abuses such as
fabricated and false confessions. Nevertheless, cases such as those of
the Guildford Four and the Maguire Seven, who were also wrongly
convicted in connection with 1970s IRA pub bombings, prompted
the Government to establish a Royal Commission to review the
criminal justice system and make recommendations for its improvement. Research conducted under the auspices of the Royal Commission
discovered that police officers had developed a number of techniques
to circumvent PACE. A favourite technique was the informal interview,
in which the officer would visit the suspect in the cell in an 'off
the record' meeting for a 'quick word', and in which he might, for
example, inform the suspect that his co-accused had confessed, or that
the police had obtained overwhelming evidence of his involvement in
other crimes but that, if he confessed, these would be forgotten. Under
PACE 1984, even informal cell visits such as this should be recorded in
the custody record sheet, but the Royal Commission research found that
custody officers would often collude with detectives by failing to record
the visits. As one leading researcher commented, 'The idea of the
custody officer as an independent check has proved chimerical' (Reiner,
1992b).

The PACE Codes of Practice on interviewing suspects were amended
in 1991 to take account of these abuses. The changes required, among
other things, that any interview taking place outside the police station
must be contemporaneously recorded, the usual method being for the
officer to make a note in his or her pocket book. However, the changes
still left scope for officers to have an 'off the record' 'quiet word' with
suspects, and pocket book notes could be as unreliable as the pre-PACE
notes of formal interviews. Crucially, PACE 1984 did not put a stop to
miscarriages of justice. False confessions obtained through oppressive
interviewing were still able to slip through the net. One such case was
that of the so-called Cardiff Three, Tony Paris, Yusuf Abdullahi and

Stephen Miller, who were jailed for life in 1990 for the murder of prostitute Lynette White. Overturning the conviction two years later, Lord Taylor LCJ said that the two detectives who interviewed Miller had done so 'oppressively', effectively brain-washing him into confessing. At the time Miller had a mental age of 11 and an IQ of just 75, which meant that he was borderline mentally retarded. His confession had in turn led to the conviction of the other two.

The central problem with police interviews, as identified by Royal Commission research, was that they were not an effort to get at the truth but rather an attempt to uncover evidence that might result in a conviction.

> 'Facts' are not elicited, they are created. The 'facts' generated during interrogation are the product of a complex process of interaction between the suspect and officer, much of which is directly traceable to the style and manner of the police questions. The creation of such facts is not an unusual or aberrant feature, but absolutely endemic to police interrogation. Nor are such 'facts' accidentally created: they are precisely what the process sets out to achieve. (McConville *et al.*, 1991)

In 1999, a major research study into interview methods ordered by the then Metropolitan Police Commissioner, Sir Paul Condon, found that the use of intimidatory and coercive tactics to secure confessions was leading to crucial evidence being excluded from court cases. Two-thirds of the cases studied involving defendants who had confessed when interviewed but who had gone on to plead not guilty at trial, resulted in acquittal because of oppressive interviewing techniques (*Guardian*, 13 September 1999).

Until 1994, suspects were cautioned that they had the right to remain silent during police interrogation, a right which also extended to any subsequent trial. The prosecution and the judge were forbidden from drawing any adverse inference from their silence. This right was an important counter-balance against the type of abuses outlined, as suspects were often very vulnerable and the police could employ a number of techniques to pressurise them into confessing. The right to silence was significantly narrowed by the Criminal Justice and Public Order Act 1994. Courts were given more freedom to draw adverse

inferences from a suspect's silence in accounting for matters such as
their possession of relevant items, their presence in a given location and
marks on their body. On being arrested suspects would be cautioned that
'You do not have to say anything, but it may harm your defence if you
do not mention when questioned something which you later rely on in
court. Anything you do say may be given in evidence.'

INFORMANTS

A further major element of detective work vulnerable to noble-cause
corruption is the use of informants. The issue is further complicated by
the fact that, even in the absence of police rule bending, investigations
can be corrupted by the informants themselves. The importance of
informants to modern policing cannot be over-estimated. According to
the Audit Commission, most crime is solved as the result of information
received from other sources (Kate Flannery of the Audit Commission,
quoted in *Daily Telegraph*, 5 September 1996). When investigating a
case, a tip-off from an informant can save the police a great deal of time
and money, and for this reason, in recent years, forces have been urged
to step up their use of informants. The Audit Commission, which has
been the source of much of the pressure, has lauded the example set by
the Hertfordshire police, who, over the three years between 1993 and
1996, trebled their number of informants to around 900. It became force
policy to make an approach to every suspect they interviewed to become
a possible source of information. Around two-thirds of the new recruits
were run by uniformed officers, a practice virtually unheard of in 1993.
Intelligence from informants led to an average of two arrests per day in
1995 (Audit Commission, 1996c).

While such statistics may appear impressive, it should be remembered that informants tend not to act out of the goodness of their own
hearts. A wide range of incentives can be offered to tempt them into
giving information, arguably the least among which is opportunity to
fulfil any latent sense of civic duty. Money is one such incentive. In 1995
the Hertfordshire informants were paid an average of £70 for each arrest
made on the basis of their information. Although some forces pay their
sources as little as £10, rewards running into thousands of pounds have
been paid to informants in some large criminal cases. In 1996, the Audit
Commission warned that some forces were not paying informants

enough (*Daily Telegraph*, 5 September 1996), but in the same year a Government-backed survey found that children as young as 13 were paid up to £300 for information. Of the 75 informant handlers, drawn from 12 police forces, who were surveyed, over 80 per cent admitted to using juvenile informants, often without notifying the children's parents. The policy was generally justified on the grounds that children under 17 are responsible for about a quarter of all detected crime (*Sunday Telegraph*, 10 November 1996). However, it has to be questioned whether witnesses of such a tender age are reliable, especially given the potential financial rewards.

Inevitably, many informants are themselves criminals and therefore, by definition, cannot be relied upon to act in the public interest. They may have ulterior motives for giving information of which the police are unaware, such as the desire to undermine rival criminals. Alternatively, the police may persuade them to trade information in return for a range of favours besides money. For example, if they are facing criminal charges, such potential informants might be promised that those charges will be reduced, or dropped altogether. If they are remanded on bail, they might be offered their freedom and the possibility of a reduced sentence when their case comes to court. Convicted prisoners can be tempted to provide information with promises of transfers to lower category prisons, where they can enjoy more privileges, and cooperating with the police can also count towards their early release on licence.

The obvious problem with all the arrangements outlined above is that the incentives are so great that the informants will be tempted to distort their accounts to fit what they think the police want to hear. The problem was dramatically highlighted by the case of Michael Stone, who was convicted in 1998 for the murders of mother and daughter Lyn and Megan Russell, who were attacked while out walking in the Kent countryside in 1996. Despite massive media coverage the police inquiry was hampered by a dearth of promising leads. Stone was not charged until well over a year after the killings, and when the case came to court it emerged that the only evidence against him was the testimony of a number of his casual petty criminal associates, some of whom he did not meet until on remand in prison. Just days after the conviction, in October 1998, one of the prosecution witnesses, Barry Thompson, who had told the jury that Stone had confessed while they were in prison together on remand, admitted that his story was 'a pack of lies'. He refused to reveal why he had lied for legal reasons, but the admission raised suspicions that he had been offered some kind of deal by the police (*Daily Telegraph*, 27 October 1998). Five months later the evidence of another key witness was also called into question. Sheree Batt told the jury that the day after the murders she saw Stone with blood on his T-shirt, but her mother Jean claimed that, prior to the trial, she had been offered a £20,000 reward, a letter to the judge to help in her appeal against a heroin conviction, and the prison of her choice if she corroborated her daughter's story. She refused because although she had seen Stone with blood on his T-shirt, she was aware of an innocent explanation for it. She believed that, having also been offered incentives to testify against Stone, Sheree had lied to the court. Stone now faces a retrial which is expected in September 2001.

Perhaps the greatest concern surrounding the use of criminal informants is that the obsession with gaining intelligence occasionally causes the police to enter into agreements with the most unsavoury criminals. Among the most notorious of recent cases is that of Delroy Denton, an illegal immigrant and well-known criminal, who was recruited by the Metropolitan Police to inform on fellow Jamaicans. In 1995, Denton raped and murdered 24-year-old Marcia Lawes at her home in Brixton, South London.

Some cases raise suspicions that officers have turned a blind eye to major crime in order to preserve their relationships with trusted informants. One such example involved Detective Superintendent Tony Lundy of the Metropolitan Police and his star informant, Roy Garner. Over the years, information provided by Garner gained Lundy some major criminal scalps and Garner an estimated £300,000 in reward money. Unfortunately Garner was himself a major drug dealer and was eventually jailed for 16 years for trafficking cocaine. Lundy appeared as a witness during Garner's trial, where he was accused by lawyers representing Customs and Excise of tipping off Garner that he was under investigation. The accusations were never proved and the only disciplinary matter brought against Lundy concerned the receipt of some fencing for his home. Lundy decided not to contest the allegation and retired on the grounds of ill health. Many were appalled by the fact that a senior detective retained a major drug dealer as an informant, but Lundy was neither the first or the last to enter into such a relationship, and to some fellow professionals his methods were justified by the convictions he obtained.

FREEMASONRY

There is no subject that causes so much anxiety in respect of police accountability and corruption than Freemasonry; an understandable reaction, perhaps, given the secretiveness with which the Craft conducts its activities. But this very secretiveness makes it impossible to gauge the influence of Freemasons within the police. Inevitably, most of the available evidence is anecdotal. For example, the former editor of *Police Review* magazine, Brian Hillyard, who researched the history of the Metropolitan Police Flying Squad, has stated, 'If you wanted to get into the squad in the sixties you almost certainly had to be a mason whatever other qualities you had. I don't think I've spoken to a CID officer of the period who wasn't a mason.'

The Masonic influence may have waned since the 1960s, but journalistic investigations in the 1980s nevertheless concluded that 20 per cent of serving officers were members of the Craft (Short, 1989) and, more remarkably, that 38 of the country's 52 chief constables were too (Knight, 1983). Masons generally scoff at suggestions that their organisation is an engine room of police corruption, and portray it as a benign upholder of civic values in general and the law in particular. It is not, they claim, a secret society but rather 'a society with secrets', and they add that 'every mason is actively encouraged to be open about his membership' (United Grand Lodge of England, 25 March 1997). They point out that the names of all grand officers are published in the Masonic Year Book, and many Masonic provinces produce similar publications which include the names of most of those who hold provincial rank.

Despite such protestations, it remains commonplace for people with unresolved grievances against the police to blame the ills of the service on the hidden hand of Freemasonry. In recent years such suspicions have occasionally been fuelled by high-profile criminal cases. For example, in the wake of the 1980 Essex bullion robbery, which was the country's biggest ever armed raid, it emerged that the raid's mastermind, Lennie Gibson, was the master of a Masonic lodge that included eight police officers. At Gibson's trial the jury heard evidence from supergrass Mickey Gervaise that police Freemasons had warned their Masonic colleagues of their imminent arrest (Morton, 1993). While he was chair of the House of Commons' Home Affairs Select Committee, Labour MP Chris Mullin stated that during his dogged campaign to uncover the truth about the Birmingham Six case, 'It became clear to me that part of the problem was there were rather a lot of Freemasons in public life in Birmingham and in a variety of professions, not just the police, who were obstructing the truth' (Home Affairs Select Committee, 20 October 1997).

In recent years the Metropolitan Police have sought to discourage Freemasonry in the ranks. Commissioner Paul Condon, who retired at the end of 1999, publicly attacked it, and a handbook for new recruits to the force advised: 'The discerning officer will probably consider it wise to forego the pleasure and social advantage in Freemasonry so as to enjoy the unreserved regard of all around. One who is already a Freemason would also be wise to consider whether he should continue as one.'

Conclusive proof of Masonically-inspired corruption has proved elusive, a function, say the organisation's critics, of its secretiveness. Mullin and his Committee argued that such criticisms would best be defused if there were greater disclosure of Masonic membership within the criminal justice system. In response, the Home Secretary, Jack Straw MP, ordered that all recruits to the various branches of the system, including the police, would have to make a declaration of masonic membership as a condition of service. He also asked all chief constables to establish public registers in which officers would be requested voluntarily to declare their membership of the Freemasons. He warned that, if the voluntary framework failed, he would introduce legislation to compel disclosure.

By May 1999, despite being reminded by the Home Secretary the previous month, only three forces had established such registers. Although the majority of chief constables were in favour in principle, only seven other forces, including the Metropolitan Police, said they had plans to do so. This slow progress caused Chris Mullin to comment: 'I recognise there are some practical difficulties, but it is clear that there is a great deal of foot dragging going on especially among the police were the masons to cooperate, they would dispel a lot of illusion. By not cooperating they create the impression that they have something to hide, which is not necessarily the case' (*Guardian*, 4 May 1999).

BLOWING THE WHISTLE

The most substantial bulwark against police corruption and malpractice should be police officers themselves, but historically few police officers have been prepared to stand up publicly against malpractice by their colleagues. 'The biggest pressure on any police officer is from his peers', says the former detective who witnessed 'noble-cause corruption' among his colleagues.

> Police officers tend to think that whatever they do — even if they're breaking the rules — is in the public interest. So they don't appreciate being told they're out of line and reporting them can be a cardinal sin. If you don't conform to the unwritten code there's a variety of ways you can be made to suffer. One of the commonest is being sent to Coventry. (former Detective Superintendent, interview by authors)

Potential whistle-blowers may be discouraged by the experience of PC Graham Cruttenden. In 1980, while serving with the City of London police, he took the brave step of reporting fellow officers whom he had witnessed stealing goods from a break-in at a clothes shop. The four officers were subsequently jailed and the sentencing judge said that PC Cruttenden deserved the 'highest praise' for his 'bravery and devotion to duty'. But such praise was not echoed by many of his colleagues, who felt that he had betrayed them. He received anonymous phone calls and veiled threats, and eventually was forced to transfer from the City of London to Hampshire police (*Guardian*, 9 March 1999).

In some cases the whistle-blower seems to fare worse than the offenders. Take, for example, PC Ron Walker of Kent police, who, as we described in Chapter 3, complained that detective colleagues were systematically massaging crime clear-up figures. After lengthy investigations by two outside forces, a detective sergeant was dismissed and 33 officers were disciplined. Whereas all these officers remained in their jobs throughout the investigations, Walker was on sick leave for almost four years. He was allowed to return to the force only if he agreed to perform routine paper work under the supervision of senior officers, rather than the type of 'hands on' police work that he favoured and for which he had received a bravery commendation. He was warned that he would face disciplinary proceedings for refusing to work if he did not do this.

A Metropolitan Police policy document on reporting wrongdoing, published in 2000, suggested that whistle-blowers who 'shop' suspected corrupt colleagues could be given new jobs, homes and even new identities to protect them from reprisals. The document, which was expected to provide the basis for a national policy, represented substantial progress in the official recognition of the difficulties faced by whistle-blowers, but it remains to be seen whether substantial numbers of officers will be prepared to undergo such drastic personal upheavals in the cause of professional rectitude (*Daily Telegraph*, 3 July 2000).

THE POLICE COMPLAINTS AUTHORITY

The examples of malpractice we have provided so far often relate to how the police handle their own affairs in relation to, for example, clear-up rates or obtaining confessions. Members of the public who might wish to formally complain about police behaviour — especially if they have been seriously injured — would by and large take their complaint to the Police Complaints Authority (PCA). In Chapter 4 we drew attention to the fact that the 1998 BCS uncovered that some 20 per cent of adults had felt 'really annoyed' by the behaviour of a police officer. The Annual Report of the PCA for 1999–2000 provides a flavour of some of the complaints made against the police during that year. For example, it (2001, at 201) describes that:

> An arrested man complained that he had been assaulted by two police officers. Town centre CCTV camera showed that the officers had kneed and punched him while lying on the ground. The supervised inquiry led to two officers being charged with assault. They each received sentences of three months imprisonment, which were suspended pending an appeal.

Similarly,

> The Authority launched a supervised inquiry after a young woman complained that two officers who offered her a lift home in the early hours suggested she would need to wear handcuffs in the police car to make it appear she was a prisoner and also for 'insurance purposes'.

One of the officers resigned shortly after this incident.

Whilst there seems to have been a satisfactory conclusion to the two incidents, the new Chairman of the PCA — Sir Alistair Graham — has made it clear that changes to the system of complaints needs to take place to improve openness, reduce timescales, increase independence and enhance accountability — all issues which have dogged the PCA since its inception in 1984, and also its predecessor the Police Complaints Board, which was set up in 1976 (Reiner, 1992a, at 236). Indeed, at the time of writing, the Home Office itself has just published *Complaints Against Police — Framework for a New System*, setting out the emerging framework for a new complaints procedure in the light of a consultation exercise undertaken by KPMG. Of note it is proposed that the PCA will be replaced by a new independent body, known as the Independent Police Complaints Commission, and have its own investigating teams, independent of the police, made up of civilian investigation managers who would manage the teams on a day-to-day basis. Additionally, it is proposed that the Secretary of State will be able to confer on non-police personnel in independent investigating teams all or part of the powers of a police constable.

6 Race

INTRODUCTION

'Everyone, irrespective of the colour of their skin, is entitled to walk
through the streets ... free from fear.'

This proclamation is from a major report into policing and race
relations. Readers might, perhaps, assume that we are referring to the
Macpherson Inquiry into the Stephen Lawrence case, but the words are
in fact drawn from Lord Justice Salmon's inquiry into the 1958 Notting
Hill riots. Over 20 years later, Lord Scarman's Report on the Brixton
riots commented that 'the history of relations between the police and the
people of Brixton during recent years has been a tale of failure'. That it
should have been necessary, at the end of the 1990s, to conduct the third
major post-War inquiry into policing and race is a depressing indictment
of the failures of the police, politicians and society as a whole to learn
the lessons of the past.

The Lawrence inquiry is the backdrop against which virtually all
discussion of policing and race in Britain now takes place. We will
therefore begin this chapter by briefly outlining the case. The police's
problems cannot be considered in isolation and, although it is beyond
the scope of this book to explore the problem of racism throughout
society in general, this chapter will briefly consider the wider context of
the rest of the criminal justice system. It will then examine the policing
of ethnic minority communities and the experience of non-white police

officers. Lastly, we will discuss the measures needed to tackle racism and assess the police service's recent progress.

THE STEPHEN LAWRENCE CASE

Stephen Lawrence, an 18-year-old black student, was stabbed to death at a bus stop in South East London on the night of 23 April 1993. Within minutes it was clear that the attack was racially motivated. His friend, Duwayne Brooks, who had witnessed the incident and had himself managed to escape only by running away, told the first police at the scene that the five assailants had shouted racial abuse. Yet the police treated the incident as an ordinary fight and, worse still, treated Duwayne, who was in shock, as hostile rather than as a vital witness and a victim. He later recalled, 'At the scene the police treated me like a liar, like a suspect instead of a victim, because I was black and they couldn't believe that white boys would attack us for nothing. They tried ... at the police station, to get me to say that the attackers didn't call us "nigger"' (*Guardian*, 25 February 1999).

Within 24 hours of the murder a number of witnesses had come forward with potentially vital information. The most important of them was a young man, later given the pseudonym James Grant, who walked into a police station and named three local teenagers — brothers Jamie and Neil Acourt and their friend David Norris — plus two other unknown youths, as the killers. The other witnesses named the two as Luke Knight and Gary Dobson. All the witnesses were frightened and wished to remain anonymous, but the police nevertheless had enough evidence to arrest the five, an action that may have yielded vital forensic evidence. But nothing was done, and the police did not regard it as necessary to commence surveillance of the Acourts' house until the weekend after the attack. On Monday, 26 April, officers observed a young white man leaving the house with what appeared to be clothing covered in a black bin liner, but no camera was available to record the event and the murder incident room was not informed. Incredibly, a full surveillance operation was not begun until the following day, because on the Monday an observation team had been deployed to watch a young black man suspected of theft. It was not until shortly before 8 pm on the Tuesday that a team was in place to observe the murder suspects, and they finished their shift after less than two hours.

It was not decided to make arrests until 6 May. Weapons, including knives, were found at the Acourts' house and in Gary Dobson's bedroom, but, despite receiving information that knives might be hidden under the floorboards, there was no evidence that the police attempted to look there. All the suspects were questioned under caution, but the interviews demonstrated a lack of planning and persistence by the police.

The handling of witnesses was also deeply flawed. Duwayne Brooks was called to three identity parades, at one of which officers accused him of stealing cans of soft drink. On another occasion, he picked out Neil Acourt from the parade, but that same day witnesses were left together in the police station without supervision, which meant that at any future trial the defence might argue their evidence was potentially contaminated and therefore inadmissible. Duwayne later identified Luke Knight, who was charged along with his four associates with murder; but according to a police sergeant who accompanied Duwayne on the identification parade, he afterwards said that he had not seen the attackers' faces. If true — and Duwayne vehemently denied the sergeant's version of events — this would mean that his evidence would be unlikely to be accepted by a court. It was therefore, perhaps, inevitable that the Crown Prosecution Service dropped charges shortly afterwards.

In a remarkable act of insensitivity, the police arrested Duwayne and charged him with violent disorder following an anti-racism demonstration. The case was dismissed by the judge on the grounds of abuse of process, but over the next few years he was arrested a further five times, with charges either not being brought, being dropped or being thrown out of court. Not surprisingly, Duwayne was convinced that the police had deliberately targeted him in order further to undermine his credibility as a witness: 'I was repeatedly stopped and searched after the murder. When the police found I had no criminal record they used other means to try and discredit me' (*Guardian*, 25 February 1999).

In 1995, Stephen Lawrence's family launched a private prosecution against the five suspects, but charges against Jamie Acourt and David Norris were dropped at the committal stage. When the remaining three came to stand trial, in April 1996, the judge ruled, as some predicted he would, that Duwayne's identification evidence was inadmissible and that the case should therefore not proceed. Even if Duwayne had been allowed to give evidence, the fact that he was suffering from post-traumatic stress disorder, due in large measure to his treatment by the police, meant he would likely have been a very fragile witness. Following pressure from Stephen's parents, the Deputy Assistant Commissioner of the Metropolitan Police, David Osland, ordered a review of the investigation by Detective Superintendent Roderick Barker. Against all the evidence, Barker eventually reported that the murder had been 'competently and sensitively investigated'. Among the catalogue of errors and omissions in the review was the failure to address why the police apparently ignored the evidence of the informant James Grant. Yet Barker's conclusions were accepted, without question, by Osland and the force's then Commissioner Sir Paul Condon.

The insult to the Lawrence family was compounded by the way they were treated by the police, in particular the failure to keep them informed of the progress of the investigation. Two officers were appointed to liaise with the family the day after the murder, but one of them had no previous experience in the role and, like many of his colleagues, was not prepared to accept that the murder was purely racist in nature. The head of the investigation, Detective Superintendent Brian Weeden, did not meet Stephen's parents until a year after the murder. He claimed to have made repeated attempts to speak with them and that they had declined an invitation to visit him at the police station. Subsequent to this, however, it became apparent that he had lost patience with both Mr and Mrs Lawrence and their solicitor.

There was no direct evidence of overt racism in the police investigation and the police's handling of the Lawrence family, but there was ample evidence of unwitting racism. It was clear that the original investigating team failed to recognise and accept racism and race relations as a central element of the investigation. Officers' attitudes to the family were often patronising, and many were unaware that their use of words such as 'coloured' and 'negro' was likely to cause offence.

Perhaps the most depressing aspect of the affair was that the truth came to light despite, rather than because of, the Metropolitan Police. As Detective Superintendent Barker's review showed, left to its own devices the force was content to draw a veil over its failings. Were it not for the remarkable determination of Stephen's parents and the support of a number of lawyers and campaigners, that review might have been the end of the story. By keeping the scandal in the spotlight — to the extent that the *Daily Mail* was driven to brand the five suspects

'Murderers' on its front page — they created the political climate in which the new Labour Home Secretary, Jack Straw, could announce, within days of coming to office in May 1997, that the affair should be the subject of a public inquiry. It was not until February 1999, almost six years after Stephen's murder, that the inquiry report of Judge Sir William Macpherson laid bare the terrible saga.

Despite the Metropolitan Police's avowed intention to cooperate fully with the Macpherson inquiry and learn the lessons of the affair, no officers were disciplined for their failings. The Lawrence family's complaints against the force were investigated by the Police Complaints Authority (PCA), which eventually found 'weakness in the leadership, direction and quality of work ... and a large number of oversights and omissions which resulted in the murder investigation failing to operate to an acceptable standard'. Five officers were singled out for criticism by the PCA, but by the time its inquiry was complete, four had retired and could therefore not be charged under the force's disciplinary code. The remaining officer, Detective Inspector Ben Bullock, faced seven charges of neglect of duty, but four were dropped by the force and, on the day that his disciplinary tribunal formally began, Bullock gave notice of his retirement, which since he had not been suspended from the force he was entitled to do. To the further annoyance of the Lawrence family, it emerged that the Metropolitan Police had argued to the PCA that Inspector Bullock should be admonished (one of the lowest penalties) rather than be fined, dismissed or demoted.

THE WIDER PICTURE

The Lawrence case was never simply about a racist murder. At its broadest it was an exploration of how Britain's public institutions treat the country's ethnic minorities. Arguably the most central (and certainly the most heated) debate to arise during the Macpherson Inquiry surrounded the term 'institutional racism'. Despite all the assurances to the contrary, there was a marked reluctance from within the service to acknowledge the problem. In giving evidence to the Inquiry, the then Metropolitan Police Commissioner Sir Paul Condon attracted huge derision when he denied that institutional racism permeated his force. The PCA inquiry also cleared the officers involved of racism.

But what is institutional racism? In his Report on the 1981 Brixton riots, Lord Scarman defined it as racism that is pursued 'knowingly as a matter of policy'. By clinging to this narrow definition, Condon and the PCA missed one of the fundamental points to emerge over the course of the Inquiry. Fortunately Sir William Macpherson did not, and he re-defined institutional racism as:

> The collective failure of an organisation to provide an appropriate and professional service to people because of their colour, culture or ethnic origin. It can be seen or detected in processes, attitudes and behaviour which amount to discrimination through unwitting prejudice, ignorance, thoughtlessness and racist stereotyping which disadvantage minority ethnic people.

Condon accepted what he called this 'new and demanding' definition as well as Macpherson's unequivocal conclusion that institutional racism was one of the factors to have marred the Lawrence murder investigation.

Background — ethnic minorities and the criminal justice system

The letter of the criminal law, of course, does not discriminate racially, but the letter of the law is not the only factor affecting a person's treatment by the criminal justice system. The agents of the system — be they police officers, prosecuting lawyers, magistrates, judges, prison governors and officers, or probation officers — are all frequently required to exercise their professional discretion. So while a decision to, for example, prosecute someone for an alleged crime is governed by the relevant criminal law, it is also influenced by the Crown prosecutor's assessment of the likelihood of the evidence securing a conviction. Likewise, magistrates and judges are required to exercise individual discretion in sentencing. All of these decisions should be influenced by such factors as official guidelines, established practice and professional experience, but they may also be affected by the individual's prejudices, be they conscious or unconscious. Official statistics offer clear evidence that racial prejudice afflicts all branches of the criminal justice system. We will deal with the police separately later in this chapter.

The most comprehensive statistics on race and the criminal justice system are published annually by the Home Office under s. 95 of the

Criminal Justice Act 1991. All these figures need to be considered in the light of the fact that non-white ethnic minorities make up around 6 per cent of the population of England and Wales aged over 10. Within that 6 per cent, around 2 per cent are of black ethnic origin, 3 per cent of Asian ethnic origin and 1 per cent other non-white ethnic groups.

The 's. 95' statistics show that in June 1998 ethnic minorities accounted for 18 per cent of the male prison population, of which 12 per cent were black, 3 per cent Asian and 3 per cent of other racial origin. Within female prisons the ethnic minority population was still higher, at 24 per cent, of which 18 per cent were black, 1 per cent Asian and 5 per cent 'other'. Ethnic minority prisoners were more likely to have been sentenced to long prison terms: 75 per cent of young white prisoners were sentenced to over 12 months, whereas for Asians the figure was 79 per cent and for black prisoners it was 89 per cent. Among adult prisoners, 47 per cent of white offenders had been sentenced to over four years, compared to 58 per cent of Asian prisoners and 63 per cent of black prisoners.

This evidence suggests that the Crown Prosecution Service and the courts deal more harshly with ethnic minority offenders than with whites, but, as the Home Office's 1999 Report acknowledged, there is a distinct lack of data concerning the prosecution and sentencing processes. The Report summarised two studies which, rather surprisingly, appeared to indicate that ethnic minority suspects might be treated more leniently. The first showed that, compared with white defendants, the Crown Prosecution Service discontinued a higher proportion of cases involving black defendants on evidential grounds and was more likely to reduce charges made against them for affray/disorder or theft. The second study, based on data collected from four pilot areas, indicated that ethnic minorities were more likely to have charges brought by the police terminated early. It also found no clear evidence of substantial differences in sentencing practice between ethnic groups at magistrates' courts. The s. 95 Report acknowledged that 'both studies raise more questions than they answer'.

The most thorough research into Crown Court sentencing was carried out in 1989 by Roger Hood, Director of the Centre for Criminological Research at Oxford University (Hood, 1992). Examining the sentences passed in over 3,300 cases heard by Crown Courts in the West Midlands, he discovered that, overall, black males were more likely to receive a custodial sentence than white males. Taking into account a number of key variables relating to the seriousness of the offence, he found that black people had a 5 to 8 per cent greater chance of going to prison. In cases of medium gravity, in which the judges had much greater discretion than in more serious cases, the difference was 13 per cent. Hood also found racial disparities in the distribution of non-custodial sentences. After taking into account various factors influencing the severity of the sentence, black adults were given higher tariff sentences than whites. For example, they were more likely to receive suspended prison sentences and less likely to be given community service or a probation order.

Hood's study concluded that 20 per cent of the over-representation of black men in the prison population was a result of differential treatment by the courts and other factors influencing the use of custody and the severity of sentence, such as being found guilty on a not guilty plea. The remaining 80 per cent was due to the seriousness of the cases involving black defendants and the disproportionate number of them who appeared in the Crown Court as opposed to the magistrates' court. These factors in turn reflected decisions made at all the previous stages of the criminal justice process.

Are ethnic minorities treated more harshly because they commit more crime? No doubt some British people believe that ethnic minorities do commit more crime than white people. Some will believe this out of blind racial prejudice, while others will recognise that, due to the wider racism in society, non-white people tend to suffer disproportionately poor education, poverty, unemployment and other factors commonly underlying criminal behaviour. In fact the available evidence suggests that ethnic minority people are no more likely to commit crime than their white counterparts. In 1995, the Home Office surveyed over 2,500 young people aged between 14 and 25, of whom 808 were from ethnic minority groups. The age group was especially significant, given that 18 is the peak age of offending for males and 15 the peak age for females. The Afro-Caribbeans in the sample group were found to have similar rates of offending to the whites, while the Asians were found to have lower rates.

There is also evidence that ethnic minority people are more likely to be the victims of crime than whites. Research conducted as part of the BCS in 1995 found that they were not only statistically at higher risk, but that they felt less safe on the streets or within their own homes. The only offences for which the Home Office requires the police routinely to record the victims' race are those involving homicide. The figures are included within the 's. 95 statistics' and again show that ethnic minorities are more likely to be victims. Of the 1,890 homicides recorded in 1996/97, 1997/98 and 1998/99, 18 per cent of the victims were ethnic minority, of which 9 per cent were black, 6 per cent Asian and 3 per cent 'other' non-white. Home Office figures show that whereas in 10 per cent of cases in which the victim was white no suspect was found, the figure was 11 per cent for Asians and 31 per cent for black people. According to the Home Office, this disparity in clear-up rates is partially explained by the fact that black people are more likely to be the victims of shootings, and that this type of homicide is generally much less likely to have suspects identified.

Whether or not ethnic minorities are over-represented at the 'receiving end' of the criminal justice system, it is certain that they are under-represented among its staff. For example:

(a)   in 1999, none of the 99 High Court judges was from an ethnic minority group, and only five of the 556 circuit judges, 17 of the 1,191 district judges and deputies, 15 of the 916 recorders, and 12 of the 403 assistant recorders were from ethnic minority groups. Six per cent of magistrates were from ethnic minorities, but only 53 of the 1,637 court clerks and deputies and only 12 of the 321 justices' clerks and deputies were from ethnic minority groups;

(b)   within the Crown Prosecution Service, 123 (8 per cent) of the 1,735 C grade lawyers were of ethnic minority, but among the 376 more senior grades of D and above there were only six ethnic minority lawyers (1.8 per cent);

(c)   only eight (0.8 per cent) of the 1,086 governor grade staff within the prison service were from ethnic minority groups and 606 (2.6 per cent) of the 23,874 officer grades;

(d)   within the probation service, 592 (9.7 per cent) of the main grade officers and 50 (3.8 per cent) of the senior grade officers were from ethnic minority groups. This represents a very significant improvement since 1989, when the respective percentage figures were just 2.6 and 0.26. At the time of writing there are no black chief probation officers, but eight members of ethnic minority groups were in senior management positions in 1999;

(e)   the legal profession has also made significant advances. In 1999, 8.4 per cent of solicitors on the roll and 8.8 per cent of barristers in private practice were from ethnic minority groups. Nevertheless, there remains strong cause for concern that the 'glass ceiling' is preventing many ethnic minority lawyers from reaching the top of the profession, and it is notable that only 2.1 per cent of QCs are non-white (Home Office, 1999).

POLICING ETHNIC MINORITY COMMUNITIES

At every location there was a striking difference between the positive descriptions of policy initiatives by senior police officers and the negative expressions of the minority communities, who clearly felt themselves to be discriminated against by the police. (Macpherson Inquiry Report)

The police service is the visible symbol of a society that fails to deliver benefits, but is perceived as being quick to deliver injustice (Home Office, 1999)

Official statistics bear out these stark portrayals of the relationship between Britain's ethnic minorities and the police, by the Macpherson Inquiry Report and HM Inspectorate of Constabulary. The statistics reflect, and no doubt to some extent explain, the wider problems of the criminal justice system described above. Since 1996, again under s. 95 of the Criminal Justice Act 1991, the Home Office has required all police forces to conduct ethnic monitoring of stop and searches, arrests, cautions and homicides.

Just over 1 million stop and searches were recorded in 1998/99, of which 94,800 (9 per cent) involved black suspects, 51,200 (5 per cent) Asian suspects and 10,000 suspects of 'other' non-white origin. Compared with 1997/98, the overall number of stop and searches rose by 2 per cent, although there was a 15 per cent drop in the number of black people stopped and a 6 per cent fall in the number of Asians. However, the falls for black and Asian people reflect sharp declines in the use of stop and searches by two forces serving large ethnic minority populations — the Metropolitan Police, where usage was down by 12 per cent, and the West Midlands, where it was down by 41 per cent (Home Office, 1999). The figures varied widely between different forces, with the highest being the Metropolitan Police where, despite the

12 per cent overall fall, over 106,000 (36 per cent) of the total 296,000 stop and searches involved non-white suspects (Home Office, 1999). Of course the ethnic minority population in London is far higher, at around 25 per cent, than in many other force areas.

When the rate at which ethnic minority populations are stopped and searched proportionate to their size is calculated, the figures are truly shocking. Nationally, the average rate for white people was 20 per 1,000, but for black people the figure was almost six times higher at 118 per 1,000 and for Asians 42 per 1,000. The figures again vary considerably between force areas. In Merseyside black people were stopped at a staggering rate of 310 per 1,000, but in Humberside the rate was only 5 per 1,000 (Home Office, 1999).

In the wake of the Lawrence inquiry the Metropolitan Police commissioned their own research into the use of stop and search in the capital. The resulting report, *Searches in London*, found that the majority of the young people interviewed did not mind being stopped and searched as long as the officer involved was polite and not 'power crazy'. As well as the 12 per cent overall fall in the use of stop and search, the racial disparities in its use had also fallen slightly. Nevertheless, the research found growing resentment among young Asians, many of whom found themselves arrested for the possession of small amounts of cannabis. The report pointed out that such tactics 'may begin to criminalise young Asian men suffering high levels of unemployment' and warned: 'There is an obvious risk that an aggressive police approach to these searches increasingly risks alienating young people from this first British-born generation, along with their peers and the cohorts following behind them.'

In 1998/99, 12 per cent of stop and searches in England and Wales resulted in an arrest. Among white suspects the rate was 11 per cent, whereas for black suspects it was 13 per cent, for Asians 12 per cent and for 'other' ethnic minority groups 14 per cent. Of the 1.33 million arrests for notifiable offences in 1998/99, 93,400 (7 per cent) were recorded as being of black people, 54,300 (4 per cent) of Asians and 12,600 (1 per cent) of 'other' non-white groups.

The average rate of arrest for notifiable offences among white people in England and Wales was 27 per 1,000 of the population, but for black people the rate was 117 per 1,000 and for Asians 44 per 1,000. Once again there were considerable variations between different forces. Cumbria had the highest arrest rate for black people at 463 per 1,000, and the joint highest rate for Asians at 102 per 1,000 (given that the county's black and Asian populations over the age of ten were estimated to be just 400 and 500 respectively, the actual number arrested would have been lower than 463 and 102). The next highest arrest rate of black people was 299 per 1,000 in Merseyside, where the black population aged over ten was estimated to be 5,800. The lowest arrest rate of black people was 46 per 1,000 in Staffordshire, which is still well above the national average rate for white people, and the lowest arrest rate of Asians was 24 per 1,000 in Norfolk (Home Office, 1999).

Of the 190,200 people cautioned for notifiable offences in 1998/99, 11,000 (6 per cent) were recorded as black, 7,500 (4 per cent) as Asian and 2,200 (1 per cent) as from 'other' non-white groups. In nearly all forces there was a lower use of cautioning for suspected black offenders than for both whites and Asians. For England and Wales as a whole, the cautioning rate for white people was 14 per cent, as against 12 per cent for black people and 14 per cent for Asians. The fact that a lower proportion of black people are cautioned rather than charged could well be a further reflection of racial bias within the police, but some criminologists have pointed out that the figures may also be a result of a higher proportion of black suspects denying involvement in the crimes for which they have been arrested (Home Office, 1999).

Unsurprisingly, given the above figures, a disproportionate number of complaints against the police — around 15 per cent in 1998/99 — are made by ethnic minorities. Of these, 8 per cent were from black people, 5 per cent from Asians and 2 per cent from 'other' non-white groups. Of the complaints of racial discrimination completed during the year, only seven were substantiated by the Police Complaints Authority. Of the remainder, 151 were informally resolved, 86 were withdrawn, 135 resulted in dispensation and 196 were found to be unsubstantiated (Home Office, 1999).

A large number of the racial discrimination complaints concerned stop and search and arrest, but a further common complaint, highlighted by the Lawrence case, is that the police have failed to respond appropriately to racial incidents. ACPO defines racial incident as: 'Any incident in which it appears to the reporting or investigating officer that the complaint involves an element of racial motivation, or any incident which includes an allegation of racial motivation made by any person.' Sir William Macpherson gave the simpler definition: 'Any incident which is perceived to be racist by the victim or any other person.' This definition was criticised by the judge who heard the case of two Leeds United footballers accused of attacking an Asian student. In ruling that the trial should be halted because of prejudicial reporting of the case in the *Sunday Mirror*, Mr Justice Poole declared that the Macpherson definition required the police to adopt an approach to such cases that was 'entirely subjective' (*The Times*, 10 April 2001).

In the past the police have been criticised for a reluctance to record racial crimes as such, but in recent years, despite débâcles like the Lawrence case, some progress has been made. In the 11 years between 1988 and 1999, the number of recorded racial incidents rose from 4,383 to 23,050, and there was a 66 per cent rise in the year up to April 1999 alone. The increases are thought to be largely due to better recording by the police and the fact that victims have been encouraged by both the police and their own communities to come forward, however, critics of Macpherson, such as Mr Justice Poole, might argue that the increase is due to the police's adoption of Macpherson's more subjective definition of a racial incident. The figures are expected to rise still further, as the recording of new 'racially aggravated' offences was not introduced until 1 April 1999.

Despite this progress, there is little doubt that there remains significant under-reporting of racial incidents. The head of community affairs in one predominantly rural force told inspectors from HM Inspectorate of Constabulary in 1998: 'I believe that we are only skimming the surface of racial incidents. For each incident reported many others probably occurred — we are only seeing the tip of the iceberg' (HM's Inspectorate of Constabulary, 1999).

A further major concern has been the number of ethnic minority suspects who have died in police custody. Most custody deaths are the result of suicide or drunkenness, but the proportion of black people who die following police action is far higher that of white people. Of the 17 people who died following police action between 1997 and 1999, seven were black, i.e., 43 per cent. By contrast, only 8 per cent of white deaths occurred in such circumstances. A Home Office report found that of the 19 deaths of black people in police custody between 1990 and 1996, nine were associated with the behaviour of the officers involved. Of the seven deaths occurring between 1997 and 1999, as of January 2000 only one was the subject of a criminal investigation (*Observer*, 9 January 2000).

Ethnic minorities in the police

At the time of the Brixton riots in October 1981, black officers made up just 0.5 per cent of the Metropolitan Police and only 0.3 per cent of the police nationally. In the wake of the Scarman Report on the riots, efforts were made by police forces nationwide to step up the recruitment of officers from ethnic minority communities. To some extent those efforts were successful, in that the proportion of ethnic minority officers rose from 0.3 per cent (HM's Chief Inspector of Constabulary, 1994) to 2 per cent in the 18 years from 1981 to 1999 (Home Office, 1999). Nevertheless, shortly before the publication of the Macpherson report, Home Secretary Jack Straw publicly rebuked eight police forces for employing fewer than ten black or Asian officers. They were, Dyffed Powys, Cumbria, North Wales, Devon and Cornwall, Dorset, Lincolnshire, Cheshire and North Yorkshire (*Guardian*, 10 February 1999). The percentage of ethnic minority residents in all of these force areas is low, varying from 0.46 per cent in Cumbria to 1 per cent in Cheshire. Ten ethnic minority officers would represent just under 1 per cent of Cumbria Police but less than 0.5 per cent of Cheshire Police.

The proportion of ethnic minority officers declines as the ranks are ascended, with such officers comprising 1.45 per cent of sergeants, 0.9 per cent of inspectors and chief inspectors, and just 0.5 per cent at the ranks of superintendent and above. As yet there have been no ethnic minority chief constables (Home Office, 1999).

So why do so few members of ethnic minorities forge successful careers in the police? There are numerous disincentives for them to join the service. Many feel that they would be shunned by their communities, most of which regard the police as institutionally racist, but probably the main disincentive is the racism they may face from within the police.

Take the case of WPC Joy Hendricks. In September 1998, this black Metropolitan Police officer, described by a former colleague as '100 per cent dedicated to the police service', finally snapped. After suffering intolerable abuse from white male colleagues, she punched and kicked one of them. She had confronted the officer — a sergeant — over earlier insults, which included being referred to as 'dodgy' — understood to mean corrupt — and 'the Stephen Lawrence Two', and demanded an apology. She claims that, rather than saying sorry, he told her, 'You're dodgy, you're bad news, you know you're bad news', and that he then made as if to hit her with a snooker cue.

WPC Hendricks was charged with assault. At her trial in August 1999, she told the magistrates' court that, from her first day, she had suffered racist and sexist abuse: 'I was treated as furniture. There they have to have a token woman, they have to have a token black — I was two for the price of one ... there was a lot of bullying, sexual harassment, racial harassment and Mickey taking. I was assaulted twice and had things thrown at me.' She also described colleagues' attitudes to black members of the public, freely expressed in front of her: '[If] they saw a white guy with a black woman they would say words like BIF, which means "black ignorant fucker".' She frequently reported such behaviour to her superiors, but no action was taken. The court acquitted her, accepting her claim that she had acted in self-defence, but, despite the not-guilty verdict, Scotland Yard said that her allegations would be investigated only if she launched a formal complaint (*Guardian*, 13 August 1999).

On his first day in the Metropolitan Police in 1973, PC Leslie Bowie was driven around in a police vehicle with a golliwog tied to its blue light on the roof. More than two decades later, despite being commended for his undercover work, he remained a constable. Repeatedly passed over for promotion, he was told he would have to work harder than his white colleagues because of his colour. In 1995 he accepted a crime squad posting to Heathrow police station, where he served under Detective Inspector Alan Garrod. PC Bowie was the only black officer in the Heathrow crime squad. DI Garrod repeatedly reprimanded him over petty issues and referred to him as 'half a person'. The ill treatment caused him to seek medical help for stress, but within two days of PC Bowie's taking sick leave, DI Garrod had written formal memoranda suggesting that he was malingering. When PC Bowie complained to senior officers, they pressed him to drop the accusations. Eventually he took the case to an employment tribunal, which in November 1999 found in his favour, declaring that DI Garrod's attempt to initiate disciplinary action was 'extreme and excessive'. Although still serving in the force, PC Bowie told the tribunal, 'I felt and still feel I don't have any confidence in the Metropolitan Police Service' (*Guardian*, 19 December 1999 and 17 February 2000).

The case of Gurpal Virdi was still more shocking. On 21 March 1991, the Asian police sergeant, with 17 years' service in the Metropolitan Police, attended what appeared to be a serious racial stabbing in West London, which had left two Asian teenagers collapsed on the pavement.

As in the Stephen Lawrence case, five white youths had carried out the attack, making racial taunts as they did so. Fortunately both victims survived, in part because Virdi was able to administer first aid treatment.

Virdi assumed that his colleagues would treat the attack as a serious racial incident — after all, the Stephen Lawrence inquiry had just begun and the Metropolitan Police were facing severe criticisms for their failures in that case — but some of the mistakes of the Lawrence case appeared to be repeated. Although three of the suspects were arrested quickly, it was left to Virdi to find the other two and recover the knife used in the attack, which had been dumped in a front garden only yards from the crime scene. Returning to duty three days later, Virdi was shocked to learn that the incident had not been recorded as a racial incident. Not only that, but detectives had failed to contact one of the victims in order to take a statement.

Despite being passed over for promotion and refused permission for other courses that white officers would be placed on as a matter of routine, Virdi had never spoken out against his employers. This time he complained that his colleagues' work had been 'sloppy', and as a result was reprimanded by his chief superintendent. Virdi was unhappy and intended to take the matter further, but before he had a chance he was arrested. Twelve officers from the Metropolitan Police's Complaints Investigation Branch scoured his house, and he was trailed by a surveillance team of the type normally employed against terrorist suspects. The CIB team said that they were searching for racist material and Virdi was told that he was suspected of sending hate mail to black and Asian colleagues in order to concoct a bogus race discrimination case. The police claimed that the messages had been printed from a computer terminal using his private log-on, but Virdi was able to establish that the material was printed when he was out of the office.

The Crown Prosecution Service did not pursue the criminal charges, but Virdi was still subjected to an internal disciplinary hearing which, in March 2000, resulted in his dismissal from the force. He immediately lodged an appeal, and the chairman of the Metropolitan Police Black Police Officers' Association branded the verdict as 'unfair, unsafe and unsatisfactory' (*Guardian*, 11 March 2000).

The outstanding disciplinary case meant that, despite being an important witness, Virdi was prevented from giving evidence against the five youths accused of the racial stabbing. In the event, only one of the five was convicted of inflicting grievous bodily harm and given a custodial sentence. Two others were convicted of affray and given probation orders, and the remaining two were acquitted (*Observer*, 6 June 1999).

Undaunted by his dismissal, Virdi took the Metropolitan Police to an employment tribunal, alleging racial discrimination and unfair dismissal. The tribunal eventually upheld the racial discrimination claim, saying that he had been treated differently to a white officer, Constable Jackie Batchelor, who was also a suspect in the investigation into the racist letters. The tribunal found that, as well as the search of his home, the force had attempted to entrap Virdi in a taped interview and failed to interview him in an informal way, as it had with PC Batchelor. It concluded: 'The explanations put forward by ... the Metropolitan Police, as representing good investigation practice are not sustainable or justifiable. We therefore infer and conclude that the reason for their failures is not incompetence but is because of Virdi's race.'

Disturbed by the parallels with the Lawrence saga, Peter Bottomley MP, in whose constituency the family of Stephen Lawrence lived, wrote of the Virdi case: 'One has to wonder about the appropriateness of deploying a team normally reserved for counter-terrorist operations in the search of an ordinary family home. I have found no report of surveillance teams being employed in similar searches involving a white officer, even in cases of suspected corruption, alleged framing of members of the public, or drugs' (*Observer*, 6 June 1999).

Conspiracies of the type alleged by Gurpal Virdi are thankfully rare, but racism of the sort he, Joy Hendricks and Leslie Bowie described is, sadly, all too routine. Moreover, Home Office research found evidence of widespread racism in the recruitment and retention of black and Asian staff. Black and Asian officers were twice as likely to resign and three times as likely to be dismissed as their white counterparts, and it took an ethnic minority officer on average 12 months longer than a white officer to be promoted to the rank of sergeant (*Sunday Telegraph*, 11 April 1999; *Guardian*, 15 April 1999).

At the core of the problem of institutional racism within the police is the attitude of its white staff. In 1997, HM's Inspectorate of Constabulary conducted a major thematic inquiry into community and race relations (CRR) issues, which resulted in a report entitled *Winning the Race*. A follow-up report published in 1999 stated:

The service has within its staff those who have been committed to laudable community and race relations principles for many years; those who have travelled their own painful path and learned from previous attitudinal mistakes; those who firmly believe they are fair in their professional dealings. This latter group, who are the majority, need to be led across the threshold to learn that contemporary policing involved the notion of treating people differently. Lastly there are those, who are the minority, whose attitudes (and at times behaviour) is such that they would be better removed from the police service. (HM's Inspectorate of Constabulary, 1999)

Far less widely reported than the Macpherson Inquiry's comments on institutional racism, this passage was equally remarkable in that it acknowledged that the majority of police officers, while not consciously or overtly racist, nevertheless need to change their approach to CRR issues.

TACKLING RACE ISSUES

In their Report on the Lawrence case, Sir William Macpherson's inquiry team made 70 recommendations. Those requiring legislative changes were addressed directly to the Government, while others demanded action at force level to address problems of police internal organisation and culture.

Many of these latter recommendations were anticipated by the Inspectorate's Report, *Winning the Race*. Like the Macpherson Report, *Winning the Race* was adamant that police forces have finally to take on board the Scarman Report's fundamental observation that 'Community relations is integral, not peripheral to policing function'. The Inspectorate made clear that the issues have to be addressed through every level of every force and, crucially, senior management have to promulgate a good practice guide which must then be strenuously and continually endorsed until the awareness of staff improves. Front-line supervisors have to follow the lead of senior management by encouraging good practice among their subordinates and intervening to deal with inappropriate behaviour and language. The CRR strategy has to be implemented throughout forces, not merely within specialist units based in areas with significant ethnic minority populations.

Among the most important of the Inspectorate's specific recommendations was that each force should conduct an audit to evaluate progress in devising and implementing a CRR strategy. Such a strategy can be effective only if the police have the confidence, trust and respect of ethnic minority communities, a tall order given the mistrust of the police within very many of those communities. The Inspectorate recognised that in order for those bridges to be built, the police would have to concentrate on improving what is known in management jargon as 'service delivery' to ethnic minority communities. Central to this process should be a recognition of the importance of community beat officers (CBOs), who are generally the first point of contact for members of the community with crime-related problems, or for those who may have intelligence that could help the police. As such, CBOs can play a vital role in enhancing the quality of life of the community in general and of ethnic minority communities in particular, which in turn cultivates those communities' confidence in the police.

Unfortunately, the performance culture foisted on the police during the 1990s (see Chapter 3) tends to rely on quantitative performance indicators, such as crime clear-up rates, rather than the qualitative, such as those delivered by CBOs. Her Majesty's Inspectorate of Constabulary recommended that the value of CBOs be enshrined in local policing plans, and that managers avoid removing CBOs from their beats in order to fulfil non-community duties.

The two principal aspects of service delivery which most affect ethnic minority communities are the response to racial incidents and the use of discretionary powers such as stop and search. The Inspectorate was clear that the Macpherson definition of a racial incident (that a crime has a racial element if the victim says it has) must be understood across the entire police service, and all officers must be aware of the importance of making the appropriate initial response to such incidents. The Lawrence case showed only too clearly the damage that can be done by officers lack sensitivity to racial crimes and failing to take the proper investigative steps. Although many forces have established specialist units to deal with racial incidents, the Inspectorate warned that it was not good enough for officers simply to note down details of a racial offence and pass them on to such units.

One of the Inspectorate's most important recommendations concerning the police's use of discretionary powers was that forces properly audit their use. Although forces have a statutory obligation to gather data on stop and searches, there is no such obligation to record the use of other discretionary powers, such as the issue of the Home Office Road Traffic Form 1 (HORT1), more commonly know as 'producer' forms, which obliges motorists to show their driver's licence and other documents at a police station. Forces should also gather such data and, more importantly, ensure that they are fed into strategic and policy decision-making.

Her Majesty's Inspectorate of Constabulary recognised that an effective CRR strategy could not be created entirely from within the police, and that it was therefore necessary to consult widely among the ethnic minority communities they served, including those elements that might be hostile to the police. As the Inspectorate pointed out, a police force's commitment to service delivery to ethnic minority communities is a major factor affecting its ability to attract and retain more ethnic minority officers, and that 'No glossy publications will bring those candidates to the door unless they are convinced that the Service is fair to their communities' (HM's Inspectorate of Constabulary, 1999). Nevertheless, in its evidence to the Macpherson Inquiry, the Inspectorate recommended that forces should be set targets for ethnic minority recruitment. It made a number of specific recommendations to boost recruitment and retention, among the most important of which was the inclusion of an ethnic minority police officer, no matter what his or her rank, on interview panels. This would ensure that cultural idiosyncrasies of language did not prejudice the candidates' chances and would help put them at ease. Candidates who did not have English as their first language could also be given help, perhaps from a mentor of similar ethnic origin, at other stages of the recruitment process, such as the initial recruitment test. The Inspectorate pointed out that such action would constitute positive discrimination, but would simply put ethnic minority recruits on a level playing field.

Ethnic minority officers could play a valuable role in other areas of the recruitment process, such as the devising of recruitment literature and advertising. Although such material is often well intentioned, the Inspectorate discovered that some ethnic minority officers found it to be patronising and misdirected, which meant that it could have the opposite effect to that intended. Retaining ethnic minority officers depends, in part, on the presence of visible role models among senior ranks and the dismantling of the 'glass ceilings' which too often prevent able officers being promoted to their deserved rank. Among the measures recommended by the Inspectorate to aid this process were the use of the Accelerated Promotion Scheme to fast-track ethnic minority graduates and the adoption by all forces of the fellowship scheme for ethnic minority graduates pioneered by the Metropolitan Police.

Removing the 'glass ceiling', increasing the recruitment and retention of ethnic minority officers, responding appropriately to racial incidents and developing a properly integrated and effective CRR strategy, all depend on effecting some fundamental changes to police culture. It is this that represents the greatest challenge to the police service and its political masters because, as the Inspectorate pointed out, the majority of officers are unaware that they need to change their approach to CRR matters.

Training officers in equality issues can obviously play a vital role in effecting the necessary changes, but the Inspectorate emphasised that this training had in the past tended to concentrate on how officers should behave towards ethnic minority colleagues. The Inspectorate recommended that in future more emphasis should be placed on the quality and equity of the service that was delivered to ethnic minority communities.

By September 1998, every police force, except Lincolnshire, had published policies on inappropriate behaviour, but the Inspectorate pointed out that such policies were meaningless unless reinforced at every command level 'in both words and action', and that effective sanctions against those who breached the policies 'must be visible and unequivocal' (HM's Inspectorate of Constabulary, 1999). A more specific recommendation was that officers' attitudes to CRR issues be taken into consideration during their annual appraisals and when they are being considered for promotion. Besides such prescriptive measures, the Inspectorate made it clear that the necessary changes to police organisational culture could take place only if the voices of ethnic minority police officers were heard, their needs responded to and their concerns addressed.

WHAT PROGRESS?

The publication of the Macpherson Report in February 1999 triggered a flurry of policy announcements, both by the Government and by the Metropolitan Police. Home Secretary Jack Straw immediately promised that the Race Relations Act 1976 would be extended to cover not only the police, but also a variety of other previously exempt official bodies, including the Civil Service, the NHS and the immigration service. When the draft Race Relations (Amendment) Bill was unveiled nine months later, it outlawed only direct racism rather than the type of indirect, institutional racism exposed by the Lawrence Inquiry which would not be open to challenge in the courts (*Guardian*, 4 December 1999). Following a barrage of criticism, led by the Commission for Racial Equality, Mr Straw amended the Bill to incorporate indirect racism.

Again in accordance with the Macpherson Report, the Home Secretary promised to set individual levels of black and Asian officers for every police force in the country, reflecting the racial make up of the local population. This would result in the recruitment of 8,000 ethnic minority recruits over the following decade. In London, for example, where 25 per cent of the population is either black or Asian, 5,662 officers would have to be recruited from these communities. At the time of the announcement the Metropolitan Police had just 865 ethnic minority officers out of a total of over 26,000. For those rural forces with very small black and Asian populations, he would set a 1 per cent base line for ethnic recruitment. Regarding stop and search, Mr Straw vowed to enact the Macpherson recommendation that suspects should be given an immediate written record and explanation by the officer involved.

The Government announced that, in line with the Macpherson recommendations, as of July 2000, a Metropolitan Police Authority (MPA) would take over much of the responsibility for overseeing the force previously exercised by the Home Secretary. Of the MPA's 23 members, 12 are drawn from the new London Assembly, four are magistrates and seven are independent members. At the time of writing seven of these 23 members are from ethnic minorities. By the first anniversary of the Macpherson Report half of its recommendations had been implemented, including race awareness training for officers and new disciplinary powers to weed out racists, but the Home Secretary conceded that the measures already in place represented the 'easy side' of the recommendations (*Guardian*, 24 February 2000).

For their part, the Metropolitan Police had set in train some of the most significant changes prior to the publication of the Macpherson Report. A new Racial and Violent Crimes Task Force was established, headed by the force's Deputy Assistant Commissioner, John Grieve. New measures to deal with such crimes were introduced to all officers in an exercise entitled 'Operation Spectrum', and 32 community safety units were established in police stations across the capital to monitor and tackle hate crimes by building bridges with community groups and developing reliable intelligence. In addition, a new lay advisory group was established to assist development of the force's handling of racial crime. Eighty per cent of the group's 50 members were from ethnic minorities and, as the Inspectorate had urged, included some of the Metropolitan Police's sternest critics.

The force attempted a more targeted and less discriminatory use of stop and search in seven pilot areas, with encouraging results. The number of stop and searches fell by 31 per cent in these areas, and at the same time the number of stop and searches resulting in arrest rose to 18 per cent. The ratio of black people to white people who were stopped and searched fell, from a previous force average of around five to one, down to three to one.

Sadly, the success of this initiative was overshadowed by figures which showed that the 12 per cent fall in the use of stop and search in London coincided with a rise in street crime. The Metropolitan Police maintained that stop and search was, in the words of Assistant Commissioner Denis O'Connor, a 'big hitter, which has a significant relationship with the volume of crime'. In fact, as the *Searches in London* report pointed out, there is little or no evidence to link the levels of stop and search with the levels of crime (FitzGerald, 1999).

Many of the Metropolitan Police's reforms were included in a larger package, entitled 'Protect and Respect', announced by Commissioner Sir Paul Condon on the day of the Macpherson Report's publication. The promised new measures included the 'fast-tracking' of racially motivated crimes through the forensic system, and new training for senior officers on race crime investigations. A new approach to stop and search would involve the monitoring of individual officers, who would be held accountable for their action. A recruitment initiative was also promised, involving a rap video aimed at encouraging young black people to join the force and the establishment of a fellowship scheme to pay the university fees of ethnic minority students who agreed to join the force. In the year following the publication of the Macpherson Report the Metropolitan Police managed to recruit 184 black and Asian officers, which raised the proportion of ethnic minority officers in the force to 4 per cent, compared to around 25 per cent of the population of London. In line with the Macpherson recommendations, the force announced plans to recruit a further 5,000 ethnic minority officers by 2009, an average of 500 a year. The pledge may have been overly ambitious, as figures released in January 2000 showed that, despite an extensive advertising campaign, only 43 additional ethnic officers were recruited in the seven months following the publication of the Macpherson Report (*Sunday Telegraph*, 16 January 2000).

Clearly, the Metropolitan Police's leadership had recognised the need to enact some of the cultural and organisational changes called for in the Inspectorate's *Winning the Race* report, but almost a year after the Macpherson Report an Inspectorate study suggested that progress on the ground had been slow. Although the study praised the Metropolitan Police as a 'beacon of excellence' in senior officers' commitment to tackling racial crime, it showed that the clear-up rate for these crimes (20 to 23 per cent) had not improved (*Guardian*, 18 January 2000).

In the wake of the Macpherson Report it was inevitable that most public attention would fall on the Metropolitan Police, but what of the wider police service? In October 1998, a year after its original 'Winning the Race' inspection and just four months prior to the publication of the Macpherson Report, the HM Inspectorate of Constabulary conducted a follow-up inspection to assess the progress that had been made on CRR matters. Despite clear improvement in some areas, the resulting report, *Winning the Race — Revisited*, made disappointing reading, with the Inspectorate observing: 'Progress has been less than satisfactory with many of the recommendations "sidelined" and few forces placing the issue high on the agenda.' Seventeen forces (40 per cent) did not have a CRR strategy in place or under development at the time of the revisit; furthermore, only 11 forces (26 per cent) had conducted a CRR audit. The inspection team discovered that many forces lacked a corporate lead in respect of CRR issues, with the result that CRR had not become a mainstream and core element of policing. In the absence of a centrally driven policy, the development of CRR strategy in these forces left too much to the discretion of the commanders of basic command units. The Inspectorate found that, while much commendable work was being carried out by some of these commanders, without the necessary lead from higher up, their good practice was not replicated across the entire force. Inevitably there was much uncertainty among officers as to who was responsible for CRR policy in their forces, and many continued to believe that CRR had a low priority. Most forces continued to undervalue CBOs, and only seven (16 per cent) formally acknowledged the contribution they made to CRR by clarifying their role and limiting their abstraction to other, non-community duties.

Her Majesty's Inspectorate of Constabulary reported that the Macpherson definition of a racial incident was still not universally understood, and that in each force there remained pockets of personal resistance to its acceptance on the grounds that it was seen as giving 'special treatment perhaps to the undeserving'. The inspectors discovered that in some forces ACPO's good practice guide in respect of racial incidents had been strenuously and repeatedly endorsed by senior management, with the result that staff awareness was much improved. In other forces, however, chief constables had effectively left the guide on the shelf.

Despite praising the many good examples of constructive efforts being made to communicate the definition of a racial incident and the appropriate responses, the Report also noted that in too many cases officers responding to racial incidents persisted in merely noting the details and passing them on to CBOs or specialist units. The inspection team also found an alarming number of cases in which a racial incident had been properly recorded by an officer, only for that definition to be rescinded by a front-line supervisor. 'This is an intolerable situation that confuses constables, represents a gross gap in knowledge or serious errors of judgment on the part of some supervisors and poses pertinent questions about the role of management', the Report commented.

Nevertheless, rapid progress had apparently been made in the rate at which the police identified cases with a racial element. In the six months between April and September 1998 the police identified 54 per cent of all such cases compared to 46 per cent by the Crown Prosecution Service, with the previous figures being 37 per cent and 63 per cent respectively (HM's Inspectorate of Constabulary, 1999).

Sadly, such figures provided little comfort to the family of Harold and Jason McGowan, a black uncle and nephew who were found hanged in Telford, Shropshire in July 1999 and January 2000 respectively. Despite the fact they had received racial threats and that the week before his death Harold told West Mercia police he was in fear of his life, the force ruled out suspicious circumstances and treated both deaths as suicides. So unhappy were some of their family at the failure to investigate the deaths as possible racial murders that they urged the Home Secretary to hand the case to the Metropolitan Police. The episode underlined that the lessons of the Stephen Lawrence case had yet to percolate through to every police station in the country.

The Inspectorate's second inspection highlighted further, albeit less dramatic, failings. The inspectors found that very few forces had adopted such standard means as weighted surveys, managerial dip-sampling and quality assurance techniques to monitor their response to victims and their investigative standards. In some forces consultation with local ethnic minority communities was found to be little more than routine, and concern was expressed that too narrow a cross-section of those communities was consulted. The inspectors also discovered that too few forces used stop and search data and other data relating to discretionary powers, to feed into their strategic and policy decision-making.

At the time of the original 'Winning the Race' inspection in 1997, 37 forces (86 per cent) had policies and practices in place actively to encourage recruits from ethnic minority communities, and a further two had plans which were at the policy design stage. Only four had no such policy, nor a current intention to establish one. But behind these generally encouraging statistics the inspectors found that there was still much progress to be made. *Winning the Race — Revisited* noted that, despite displaying the will to make progress, some forces were not prepared 'to face the uncomfortable process of questioning their own established approach to recruitment'. Most forces had neither a programme of positive action to place would-be ethnic minority recruits on a level playing field with their white peers, nor any ethnic minority input into the recruitment process.

In the year following the publication of the Macpherson Report, more than a third of forces had failed to recruit a single black or Asian officer, and the number of ethnic minority officers had fallen in nine of the 43 English and Welsh forces. Of the 260 black and Asian officers recruited in England and Wales, 184 were recruited by the Metropolitan Police alone, which meant that just 76 were recruited by the remaining 42 forces combined (*Guardian*, 24 February 2000).

The Inspectorate's second inspection discovered that 27 forces (63 per cent) had systems in place to monitor the retention of ethnic minority staff, compared to only 19 (45 per cent) in December 1997. The inspectors expressed concern that 12 forces still had no such arrangements. Of the forces visited, ethnic minorities accounted for 3 per cent of all appointments, but 5 per cent of all voluntary resignations and 8 per cent of all dismissals. There was little evidence of ethnic minority officers breaking through the 'glass ceiling'. In the previous three years, no ethnic minority graduates had found a place on the Accelerated Promotion Scheme. In 1998, only 85 such graduates applied to the Scheme, which was just 6.4 per cent of the total, and of those, only one progressed beyond the force selection stage to the extended interview process.

Addressing the thorny problem of the organisational culture of the police, *Winning the Race — Revisited* concluded that despite moving in the right direction, it was not moving quickly enough. The original inspection report commented on the lack of intervention by sergeants and inspectors to deal with inappropriate behaviour or language from their subordinates. On its revisit the Inspectorate team found only marginal improvements to this front-line supervision. Focus groups of ethnic minority officers assembled for the purposes of the revisit reported that there had been changes for the better since the 1980s, but the inspectors noted that there were 'still too many accounts of distressing behaviour or, at best, managerial indifference to ethnic minority staff'. The Report went on:

> Frequently during the revisit there were accounts of ethnic minority staff raising issues of inappropriate language and behaviour of colleagues, supervisors or managers towards them. Sadly there was a too common experience of management failing to treat their concerns seriously and, in isolated incidents, 'turning' the complaint against them. Even when the matter was investigated they were left unsupported in the lengthy process and often felt ostracised from the organisation. (HM's Inspectorate of Constabulary, 1999)

The Inspectorate found that some progress had been made in testing officers' attitudes to policing diverse communities at the selection, promotion and annual appraisal stages. Whereas the original inspection found that just seven forces (16 per cent) had identified testing procedures, by the time of the revisit 29 (67 per cent) explicitly tested for these attitudes during selection, 35 (81 per cent) during promotion procedures and 19 (44 per cent) in annual appraisals. However, the inspectors found that 11 forces (26 per cent) still had no programme of CRR training in place for their staff. The Report commented: 'As the service approaches a new millennium, with nearly 20 years since the publication of the Scarman Report, it is disappointing to see so many forces failing to address this issue.'

Her Majesty's Inspectorate of Constabulary expressed concern about the type of training on offer. Too often it tended to concentrate upon internal equal opportunities issues, rather than on external service delivery. Few forces were found to have completed a training needs analysis tailored to suit the demands of their particular locality and staff. Many programmes focused purely on officers' attitudes and cultural understanding, rather than on practical matters such as properly understanding the ACPO definition of a racial incident and the use of stop and search powers.

The Inspectorate's findings were dramatically underlined by the managing director of one of the companies appointed by the Home Office to train forces in community and race relations. In an interview with the *Guardian* newspaper on the anniversary of the Macpherson Report, Dainna Yach of Ionnan said that an overwhelming majority of officers had a problem with race, and some 'don't see black people as individuals'. Having worked with eight forces, she concluded:

Two thirds of police officers have a problem addressing the race issue, either because of ignorance, confusion or being difficult. I supposed, based on the feedback we've had, one third are very resistant to change. They don't think there is a problem, they can't see the connection between race equality and service delivery. A third are confused and resentful but not actively resistant. A third are switched on and are willing to learn. (*Guardian*, 24 February 2000).

CONCLUSION

It is to be hoped that the publication of the Macpherson Report and the various initiatives that came in its wake will accelerate the lamentably slow pace of change observed by HM's Inspectorate of Constabulary. Policing and race must remain high on the political agenda and the necessary legislative and organisational changes brought to fruition, but these changes can be effective only if the minority of overtly racist officers are weeded out of the police service and the majority of the remainder recognise the need to alter their approach to race issues. In turn, we must recognise that the police cannot be considered in isolation:

racial prejudice must be addressed throughout all our public institutions and wider society. It is perhaps only when such profound changes have occurred that Britain's ethnic minorities will begin to trust the police completely.

7 Cop Culture

INTRODUCTION

This chapter is concerned with the debate about the existence of a 'cop culture'. By this we mean the idea that there is a distinct and identifiable set of beliefs and assumptions (sometimes also described as a 'canteen culture') which determines how the police will behave not just in the canteen but also operationally out in the streets. Every organisation has a culture (both formal and informal) that to a greater or lesser extent makes it distinct. Yet the search for — and some would claim the discovery of — a cop culture is seen as being more important than the discovery of, for example, the 'canteen culture' of academics, computer programmers or accountants, because of the unique role played by police officers in our society. Put simply, police officers have great discretionary powers over other individuals to stop them in the streets, search them and, in certain circumstances, to have them arrested. (No matter what might be claimed for academics, computer programmers or accountants, they do not have the same discretionary powers.) More-over, this discretionary authority to exercise lawful power is devolved to the lowest level of authority. In most policing situations it is the patrolling officer — often the officer with the least operational experience, or experience of life — who is asked to exercise discretion in his or her dealings with the public. So how officers behave, how they express themselves, the sorts of jokes that they tell, which organisations they belong to and so forth, are all seen as important indicators of how these officers will react to operational situations. If the officer is racist, sexist or aggressive in the canteen, he or she is also likely to be so out on patrol.

In this chapter we attempt to unravel the existence or otherwise of what constitutes 'cop culture' (racism within the police is discussed in detail in Chapter 6). In doing so, we first review the secondary literature on this issue, which of late has become far more lively with the publication of Waddington's (1999) 'appreciation' of cop culture. In it, Waddington swims against the tide of most sociological research in this area, which has hitherto seen 'cop culture' as almost overwhelmingly a 'bad thing', and instead attempts to offer explanations for its existence in more positive terms. Secondly, we have interviewed a variety of police officers concerning their views about 'cop culture', and these interviews form the basis of the chapter. The interviewees were all chosen because they were known to the authors, either as former colleagues or as students, and were promised anonymity. Each was felt to offer a distinct insight into 'cop culture' as a result of his or her age, sex, sexual orientation or race, and some general biographical details are provided below. Lastly, we have triangulated the information gleaned from these interviews in a variety of ways — from visiting police stations, eating in police canteens and riding in police cars, to using Internet discussion groups and web sites catering for, for example, gay and lesbian police officers.

A BRIEF ACCOUNT OF 'COP CULTURE'

It is Reiner (1992a) who has perhaps been the most vocal proponent of the existence of a distinct 'cop culture'. For example, he maintains that 'an understanding of how police officers see the social world and their role in it — "cop culture" — is crucial to an analysis of what they do, and their broad political function' (Reiner, 1992a, at 107). He goes further and also suggests that this culture shapes police practice. In doing so he echoes other researchers in this area, for example Brogden, Jefferson and Walklate (1988, at 33), who claim that 'in the canteen, in the slack hours of the early morning, as well as under pressure on the street, the junior officer learns about the job, and the accepted ways of dealing with practical situations'. However, perhaps the earliest proponent of a distinct cop culture was Skolnick (1966), who suggested that police officers developed a 'working personality' as a response to two variables within the police role — danger and authority — both of which had to be seen within the context of needing to appear efficient, or, more simply, to get results. This notion of 'danger' relates to the unpredictability of police work rather than, for example, the dangers associated with working with asbestos or explosives. Rather, the danger came from the unknown and potentially volatile situations with which the police were asked to cope, and the fact that it was difficult to predict which situations would be dangerous. 'Authority' here is meant to convey the sense that police officers have the potential to exercise legitimate force — power — and that they come to symbolise the rule of law itself.

Skolnick's work is clearly dated and fails to take into account the diversity of police cultures that exist between countries, forces, ranks, and even officers of the same rank performing different roles. In short, Skolnick seems to paint with broad brush strokes, and it has been left to others to fill in the detail of how this 'cop culture' operates in less monolithic and static terms. Robert Reiner (1992a, chap. 3) in particular has added immeasurably to our understanding of this issue, largely through interviewing police officers of various ranks in different forces. He suggests that the main characteristics of 'cop culture' are as follows:

- mission–action–cynicism–pessimism
- suspicion
- isolation/solidarity
- conservatism
- machismo
- prejudice
- pragmatism.

Given the importance of these characteristics to an understanding of cop culture, we will spend some time in outlining Reiner's argument.

Reiner suggests that a central feature of cop culture is a sense of 'mission'. Put simply, that being a police officer is not simply just another job, but one that has a worthwhile purpose, protecting the weak from the predatory. The police form a 'thin blue line', protecting civilisation from the forces (whatever they may be) which threaten its destruction. As such they are indispensable. Inevitably this involves action, and Reiner, like Holdaway (1983), stresses that there are aspects of the police's job which are hedonistic, exciting, and 'thrill-seeking', such as legally driving high-performance police cars at very high speeds. These occasions may be rare, as most police work is rather routine and often boring, but opportunities for the 'chase, the fight and the capture' obviously exist. Nevertheless, police officers often develop views which are cynical and pessimistic — they have 'seen it all before', and each new trend or fashion is viewed in apocalyptic terms, with the potential to destroy the moral world that has shaped the sense of mission that the police have developed.

Police are trained to be suspicious — to look for signs of trouble, clues and potential danger. The worry here is that this suspicion leads a police officer to stereotype potential offenders, and that this stereo-typing becomes a self-fulfilling prophecy. Thus a disproportionate number of young black men get stopped and searched in the streets, inevitably leading to more young black men being arrested, which in turn 'confirms' the stereotype that young black men are more likely to be criminal. Allied to this, as most police are socially isolated given the nature of their job and the shifts and hours that they work, there is little likelihood that they will encounter, for example, young black men who enjoy playing the piano, reading books, or who might wish to become police officers themselves. Similarly, the need to be able to rely on one's colleagues in a 'tight spot' means that a great deal of internal solidarity exists, which does little to erode the sense of isolation from other members of society that police officers may experience. However, Reiner is also correct to point out that there are conflicts within the police organisation, based on rank, the nature of the job being done (for example between uniformed or detective branches) or between different force areas. Reiner suggests that there are differences between 'management cops' and 'streetwise' operational officers, with the former having to present a more legalistic and rational face to the public, while the latter may feel that they have to bend the rules to achieve results.

The police tend to be conservative both politically and morally. Furthermore, the nature of their organisation is hierarchical and disciplined and, as Reiner puts it, this means that a 'police officer with a conservative outlook is more likely to fit in', which in turn is amplified by the process of selection and promotion (Reiner, 1992a, at 122).

Reiner further suggests that police officers tend to be conservative on moral and social issues, and thus, for example, would dislike groups such as drug takers and homosexuals, who would be seen as challenging conventional morality. This is not meant to imply that 'cop culture' is puritanical. Rather, it is dominated by what Reiner describes as 'old fashioned machismo' — with high divorce rates, stress and hard drinking as evidence of over-indulgence in the pub after a shift has ended. Indeed, one of the authors remembers having to change his drink to gin and tonic so that he could drink tonic water without the gin, thus camouflaging his drinking habits from his more hard-drinking colleagues.

One of the most worrying aspects of the conservatism of 'cop culture' has been alluded to earlier — racial prejudice (see Chapter 6). Reiner used his own research from Bristol in the early 1970s to suggest that the police were hostile to and suspicious of black people. He quoted one officer as saying: '... the police are trying to be unbiased in regard to race relations. But if you asked them you'd find 90 per cent of the force are against coloured immigrants' (Reiner, 1992a, at 126). More recent research would confirm these statements — in particular that of Holdaway (1983) and Brogden, Jefferson and Walklate (1988) — although, as Reiner suggests, racially prejudiced views do not necessarily have to form the basis for operational action out on the streets. However, the murder of the black teenager Stephen Lawrence and the police handling of that investigation again drew attention to how the police dealt with the black people with whom they come into contact.

The last aspect of 'cop culture' to which Reiner draws attention is pragmatism. By this he means the simple desire that a police officer has to get through the day as easily as possible. A police officer does not want fuss — especially paperwork — and would rather stress the practical, no-nonsense aspects of the job. Reiner describes this as 'conceptual conservatism' (Reiner, 1992a, at 128), given that this pragmatism often masks an atheoretical culture which dislikes research, innovation and change. Indeed, in conducting the research for this chapter, one of our original subjects — a former student who was going through his initial police training having completed his undergraduate degree — withdrew from the project because, as he told us, 'they don't like research, and if I continue to help it will look bad for me'.

APPRECIATING 'COP CULTURE'

While other researchers might stress different issues — such as police attitudes towards female or black police staff, or the differing cultures of the Special Patrol Group, or community constables — all of which have added to our understanding of 'cop culture', few would disagree with the basic picture painted by Reiner. In particular, most researchers would see this culture as essentially negative, given that it seems to encourage many routine injustices and makes the police resistant to change. However, Waddington (1999) takes a different view and offers an 'appreciative' conception of 'cop culture'. In particular, he attacks previous conceptualising on this issue, given that there has been an implicit assumption that 'talk' leads to 'action'. In short, that 'if the police act in a racist fashion when performing their duties, this can be readily attributed to racist motives produced and sustained by racist canteen banter' (Waddington, 1999, at 288). Waddington denies this 'conceptual bridge', arguing that what police officers say and what they do are largely determined by the context in which they find themselves, rather than the culture that might develop in the canteen. Thus he argues that if 'there is little relationship between the privately expressed views of police officers and their actual behaviour on the streets, it appears that the concept of a police sub-culture contributes little to the explanation of policing' (Waddington, 1999, at 289).

Nonetheless, in developing his own 'appreciative' understanding of 'cop culture' Waddington does accept that a police sub-culture exists, and indeed he argues that this sub-culture is similar in police forces throughout the World. He contends that its existence 'is a rhetoric that gives meaning to experience and sustains occupational self-esteem' (Waddington, 1999, at 295). The components of this sub-culture relate to: (i) the police being the custodians of state authority, which inevitably means that policing is a 'conservative vocation'; (ii) the fact that that authority is backed with potential force, and thus the 'glorification of action and excitement'; (iii) the fact that this in turn leads to a 'cult of masculinity' and 'isolation' from other members of the public; (iv) a 'sense of mission' which comes from the fact that the police 'dignify' their work, which is often 'dirty work', with sections of the population who are regarded as 'outsiders' and whom the police thus find it easier to 'denigrate'; and (v) the 'defensive solidarity' of the police — a recognition of their 'precarious position' in society (Waddington, 1999, at 295–302).

Yet if, as Waddington argues, this sub-culture — which does not seem to differ markedly from the research that he had been quick to challenge — is merely a 'palliative' rather than a guide to action out on the streets, how do we explain how the police behave operationally? He claims that much of the police's behaviour can be explained as a desire to 'avoid trouble' in 'the circumstances in which they act' (Waddington, 1999, at 302). However, while it is fair to argue that what one says and what one does are not necessarily the same things, and that aspects of police sub-culture can clearly be seen within the broader cultural map of the country, we still have to be able to explain police behaviour beyond the simple desire to 'avoid trouble', especially as this phrase implies that their role is purely reactive. Similarly, 'circumstances' and 'context' are not fixed entities, but change on a regular basis according to the people — the *dramatis personae* — who find themselves within those circumstances and contexts within which policing occurs. Is it really unreasonable to presume that there is a bridge between what a police officer says and how he or she socialises which moulds that officer's response to how situations will be policed operationally? Would one police officer behave differently from another depending on that police officer's background, sex, age, race, rank and experiences within the police? For while Waddington is right to push the debate about 'cop culture' beyond a simple desire to paint the police as racist, sexist thugs, in 'appreciating' this culture too readily he fails to consider the potential it has for guiding police action.

COPS TALK ABOUT 'COP CULTURE'

In attempting to test how far this potential went, we conducted a series of interviews with eight serving and two former police officers from a variety of ranks and both sexes in differing forces, with different ethnic backgrounds, ages, educational qualifications, and sexual orientations, about their experiences of 'cop culture'. All were promised anonymity, although one — Detective Inspector Howard Groves of the Metropolitan Police — gave a public talk at the University of Central England followed by an interview, and was happy to be identified. Each interviewee was known personally to the authors either as a former colleague, or as an ex-student, or through other non-police operational contact, and it is accepted that this may have affected what was said, although we attempted to triangulate the information which was supplied in a variety of ways. Each interview took place outside of the place where the officer worked if he or she was still serving, and a typical interview lasted about two hours, although some lasted much longer. Wherever possible we tried to confirm what was being described through official records, related web sites and what we could observe in our own academic dealings with the police. Consequently, we visited numerous police stations, and took part in three police operations during 1999 in Derby, Lancashire, and Devon and Cornwall. Participation in these events allowed us to go on patrol with officers, knock on doors, observe police–public contact (including motorists being stopped and asked for identification and related documentation), ride in police cars and socialise after the end of a shift. It should also be remembered that one of the authors was a serving police officer for some 30 years, and his experiences also contributed to our ability to triangulate what was being observed or described in interview.

As May has commented, 'interviews yield rich insights into people's experiences, opinions, aspirations, attitudes and feelings' (May, 1993, at 109). Nonetheless, we do not claim that these interviews offer a comprehensive picture of 'cop culture'. As with most ethnographic research, we are merely interested in deepening our understanding of what has been described as 'cop culture' to determine how and when it operates so as to comprehend its subtleties and complexities. Thus we deliberately chose to interview officers who were female, Muslim, Afro-Caribbean or openly bi-sexual, not only because they might be able to throw light on 'cop culture' in general — although clearly they were not a 'representative sample' — but also to discover how they made sense of that culture given their race, sex, or sexuality. In particular, we wished to examine the relationship between 'saying and doing', so as to determine how far talk in the canteen becomes operational practice out on the streets. In contrast to Waddington's scepticism, those officers to whom we spoke were unequivocal about their opinion on this matter. As one officer of six years' standing put it, 'the banter in the canteen is how we behave on the streets'.

Of note, this same officer suggested that the phrase 'canteen culture' was misleading, given that the attitudes and prejudices of his colleagues did not surface so much in the canteen — perhaps because remarks would be so easily overheard — as in other places. He suggested that, 'there's less of a "canteen culture" in terms of the canteen, and the culture is more dominated by being in a car with a mate as part of a crew. Now that's only two of you, but in a PSU (Police Support Unit) you will have up to six altogether — and most will share a pretty common outlook, so that the banter is on a pretty communal level'. Some support for this observation came from Detective Inspector Howard Groves, who 'remembered [in the early 1980s] sitting in the van watching a black woman taking her child to church. A colleague said ''I bet when she's finished she'll throw a few bottles'''.

For ease of presentation we will outline extracts from these interviews based on the variables of 'cop culture' as defined by Reiner, and short biographical details about the interviewees are offered at the beginning or end of each extract. However, as these were 'open' interviews, we did not attempt to construct the interviews around Reiner's definitions, and instead preferred to allow the interviewees themselves to describe what they viewed as 'cop culture'. Often this did conform to the picture painted by Reiner, but on other occasions new material emerged, sometimes of a quite startling nature. So as to preserve anonymity — and it should be remembered that the majority of those officers that we interviewed are still serving — those biographical details that are offered are very limited and generally consist only of descriptions related to age, sex or rank. Where it is relevant we have drawn attention to more specific biographical detail, such as sexuality, race or religion. We do not identify the force in which the officer served, although it should be noted that we conducted interviews with police from a range of forces serving a variety of communities.

A sense of mission

All those interviewed described joining the police because it was 'different' from other jobs. This 'difference' was described in a variety of ways. However, the most common way of expressing it was to say that being a police officer was 'a little different from the norm. After all I've put away a couple of murderers and paedophiles — that's got to be a good thing really' (former detective inspector (DI), 44). A still serving officer of six years' service thought that being a police officer was a 'worthy profession for someone who wasn't academic ... as a child I viewed the police as having awe and respect, so in joining I felt that it would give me social standing, and my parents would be pleased'. He continued that he thought that 'the role — the organisation — made me think that I was doing a good job'. Thus this social standing came from the work that the police were being asked to do, and from the authority that they had as a consequence. These same themes were common to all interviewees, whether they were Muslim, Afro-Caribbean or female. One female ex-officer who had had four years' service said that she had joined because 'it seemed like a worthwhile thing to do'. As Howard Groves — an Afro-Caribbean Detective Inspector — describes it, 'I joined because the police were people that got respect when I was growing up, and I would say that I wanted that respect too'. Even so, he pointed out that he 'had to satisfy myself that in joining my friends wouldn't disown me, and so I had to get them all together and tell them — by and large they were positive'.

When pushed about why this respect would be given, one interviewee talked about 'the power thing' (officer, 30). He described 'a collective ethos among many new officers that you can compensate for inadequacies by putting on a uniform and being in charge. Ineffectual, inconsequential people, with no social dynamic, could literally transform themselves by putting on a uniform, which gave them a sense of power'. The former DI added that he joined because he was 'bored with trains' (which he used to drive), and there was 'an air of power and respect. Yeah power — a sense of power, and of doing something different from your friends. In today's terms it was a "cool job"'. Power was closely associated with action by the interviewees. As one put it (male, 30), 'the fact that those blue lights and the siren goes and it's 80 miles per hour, and you are flying to an incident where *you* matter and you have this allowance that no one else has to break the law is just funny stuff'. This sense of action was confirmed by both female interviewees, although interestingly it was these interviewees who were most willing to volunteer that 'it isn't action all day you know ... in fact it's often really boring'. Female staff seemed to also exercise other operational cultural roles, and one of the authors witnessed some female staff attempting to defuse a potentially volatile situation, which was being exacerbated by a male colleague who was eager to make an arrest. In pursuit of action, the former DI chose to work on the Special Patrol Group (SPG) of the Metropolitan Police when he was 21: 'The SPG was the elite of the uniform branch ... you were the riot squad. It was fights, fights, fights. You flooded areas that had high crime rates, and so I did SWAMP '81. It was very professional, not a cowboy outfit.' When the SPG was disbanded, he joined the CID, and thereafter the 'Flying

Squad', so that his entire career was dominated by the same desire for action-centred activity. Indeed, he resigned because he was 'going to have to wear a funny hat again — you know, go back into uniform'. Perhaps unsurprisingly, he is now employed as a bodyguard.

The opposite of action is, of course, the boredom that comes from routine, and we had an opportunity to witness how some police officers deal with that boredom first hand. Taking part in an operational exercise in Devon and Cornwall aimed at catching deer poachers — which had become big business as a result of the BSE scare — one of the authors found himself sitting in a powerful Range Rover with two traffic police officers who were attached to the exercise. As the hours passed into the early morning and it was clear that there was very little activity, one of the officers pronounced himself 'absolutely bored and fed up', and with that proceeded to stop any vehicle that was on the road and then demand to see what the driver had in the boot of the car. When this too became less than interesting — for nothing untoward was found — the two traffic police decided to 'raid a gypsy camp' some ten miles away from where the exercise was supposed to be based. This raid — in the very early hours of the morning — netted a small amount of cannabis and one arrest.

Prejudice

The identification of a gypsy camp as being suitable for a raid is, of course, related to the stereotyping of certain sections of the community as being criminally orientated. One of our interviewees explained that this happens as a result of the fact that 'policemen hate criminals, and in [named area] we hate heroin addicts and young offenders — who are usually heroin addicts. So you constantly target and stereotype. A youth in a black bomber jacket and black trousers late at night will definitely get turned over — it's a stereotypical target. We can't help it' (officer, male, 30). Other interviewees described it as a 'fight between "us" and "them"'. Clearly there has been a great deal of research about how black people are policed, and whether they too suffer from the stereotyping that is being described above. Indeed, the same interviewee explained that there were so few black people in his area that this was not an issue, but Detective Inspector Howard Groves volunteered his own experiences on this matter:

I've been stopped four or five times myself. I'm certain that I was stopped because I drove a Ford Capri. I remember once I had just driven from my home to the end of the road, and I saw a police car. I knew that I was going to be stopped. I automatically slowed down so that I knew that I was within the speeding limit, but I didn't show my warrant card when I was stopped. The Officer said 'this your car mate?' He asked where I lived, and I said 'where you've just seen me come from'. I asked why he had stopped me, and he said 'oh don't worry about that', and I just started to laugh. So I said that I work at the police station, and he said 'what, in the canteen?' 'No', I said — 'I'm one of you', and he said 'what, a civilian?' Again I asked him why he had stopped me, and then I showed him my warrant card. He examined it carefully and slowly as if he couldn't believe his eyes. Now that was twenty years ago, but it is still happening.

Detective Inspector Groves then explained why he believed it was 'still happening', based on his recent experiences of being in charge of a murder case in London:

I'm first on scene, and so I have to decide if it's suicide or murder. As we waited for the murder squad to turn up, we — me and some of my officers — were monitoring the scene. Then the first officer from the murder squad turns up — he had his hand in his pocket, and he was chewing gum. He walks up to one of my staff and asks 'who's in charge'. The officer nods in my direction, and the officer from the murder squad looks me up and down, and says 'what him?!'. My colleague walked off and just shook her head. At that point, the Inspector from the murder squad turns up, and he asks the same question. I get looked up and down again, and he too walks off and starts talking to my sergeant. I was given no respect from a colleague of the same rank, and this incident really did make me think as to whether anything has actually changed since the 1980s.

What should be remembered here is that Detective Inspector Groves was talking about an incident that occurred after the publication of the Macpherson Report, which had drawn attention to the institutional racism of the Metropolitan Police, and that the racism that was being described related to racism between members of the same force and of the same rank. He went on to describe how other staff with whom he works generally treat him, and was quick to point out that it had been his white staff who had reported the incident regarding the murder squad detectives to his superiors. He said, 'most of my colleagues think that I'm all right. I'm a 'top man', but then I have to point out to them that they don't know other black staff or other black people. They have preconceived views and so in my 20 years I not only feel that I have to prove myself as a policeman, but also as a black man.' He went on to amplify this statement by describing what happened after he had passed his inspector's exam: 'When I passed my exam people said that I got through because of some "quota". They might not have been racist, but there was a perception that I got promoted because of my colour. That made me very resentful. I had worked my butt off for it, and eventually I think I've changed people's perceptions about what a black police officer can achieve.'

In interview other prejudices also emerged not only about which sections of the community needed 'watching', but also internal operational prejudices about who was a 'good copper'. The two female officers, for example, described numerous sexist practices, jokes and innuendoes, and one (who has had four years' operational experience) thought that her working environment had changed only when a female sergeant had taken over. One male officer commented that colleagues 'judge the women by their "blokiness" — their ability to get stuck in, and their sickness record. They [i.e., male police officers] seem to have a difficult time remembering that at home they have a wife, and at work they have a colleague who is female, wears trousers and has handcuffs. Frankly, they'd rather have a male colleague — it's like a bible fable that if you are in "the bundle of bundles" don't be with a woopcee [literally a WPC]'. The former detective inspector remembered that in the early 1990s the Flying Squad had taken a rare female recruit: 'No one was sexist towards her, but she was just useless — she didn't have any informants, or pavement jobs' (a bank robber arrested on the pavement outside of the bank).

Machismo

Clearly this prejudice is related to the perception that policing is a 'man's job', and machismo within the culture is promoted and accepted. The former detective inspector put it quite bluntly when he described his colleagues as a 'hard drinking lot — no teetotallers or vegetarians

— they were a good bunch of blokes'. Indeed, he described himself as 'not a "nineties man" — the Richard Madeley type, talking to women about cellulite and make-up — bloody Hell!'. One male interviewee who is openly bi-sexual described the culture as having 'a macho element because the job is macho. It has to be that way to perform. ACPO [the Association of Chief Police Officers] is making huge efforts to stamp out racist and sexist behaviour, but the people in ACPO used to be the culture that they are trying to stamp out'. When pushed about how his colleagues regarded him as a result of his own sexuality, he explained that in one sense he had been 'outed' accidentally, as opposed to choosing to come out to his colleagues, and that as a result he felt resentment that he had become 'public property', which had turned him 'into a freak — a circus side-show'. Indeed 'GayPolice.com', a web site for gay, bi-sexual and lesbian police, is filled with stories about 'coming out' at work, and seeking advice about how to handle this issue. The site also allows gay and lesbian staff to contact each other, and perhaps some measure of the culture of 'coming out' can be gleaned from the fact that of the eight police officers seeking partners through the site in May 2000, all described themselves as 'straight-acting', or a 'man's man', emphasised the need for discretion, and two described themselves as married 'but gay'. The Lesbian & Gay Police Association web site — which was formed in 1990 but has 'grown to include members in nearly every UK Police Service' — offers gay and lesbian staff advice and support, and states that it works towards promoting better equal opportunities for lesbian and gay police, and better relations between the police and the gay community.

Just how all of this goes down in the day-to-day practice of policing is difficult to determine, but clearly female, gay and bi-sexual staff explicitly challenge the machismo of the dominant culture. The officer who is openly bi-sexual, for example, felt that his sexuality had not become 'an issue' partly as a result of his being a 'custody officer'. It is worthy of note that an openly gay officer also worked in custody. In short, both were hidden from public view — where 'the real policing takes place'. When asked why he had volunteered for this posting, he stated that he had done so to 'escape', but found it easier to describe his gay colleague's reasons rather than his own: '. . . the gay guy's been through a Hell of a time having to come to terms with who he is. He's sensitive, and struggles long and hard, and he now feels safer in custody. Each day is the same. Nothing shocks you, and you are not on public display'. However, he felt that his bi-sexuality had affected 'almost every relationship with male and female colleagues'. He admitted that 'I have quite a camp style to me, but I am comfortable with that — more so than this machismo bollocks. In a way I'm simply treated as a novelty, but no one doubts my balls about getting stuck in'.

Heterosexual relationships were also problematic. The former detective inspector, for example, described being a 'DI' as 'Divorce Impending', and all the interviewees were either resolutely single, or had failed marriages or disastrous long-term relationships. Only the Muslim sergeant was in a stable, long-term marriage. Interviewees blamed this state of affairs on the job with its long hours and shift systems. Policing became, in the words of one of the female officers, 'all encompassing', leaving little room for anything else. Not only that, there was a 'sense of isolation from other people because of what you do. I have been introduced to other people only to feel them clam up because they are reluctant to speak because their tax disc is out of date, or they haven't paid their TV licence, and so it drives us even more inwards for our relationships and friendships' (female officer, 2 years' service). The former detective inspector had two failed marriages behind him, and was perhaps the most open about how the job had affected the relationships that he had had. Having got divorced from his first wife very early in his career — 'I think that I married her to get out of the section house' — he remarried, and eventually found himself in the 'Flying Squad'.

> I got divorced again when I was on the Flying Squad. My wife booted me out, and I knew she would. It was a choice between her or the Flying Squad. I'm selfish — I loved the feeling that I got from the Flying Squad more than I loved my wife; that feeling of power, control, and the satisfaction that you get from power and control.

When pushed about whether it was the police that had created these feelings, or whether they had always been part of his psychology, the former detective inspector was no less forthcoming. He stated that while the question was 'a hard one to answer', 'I was emotionally selfish anyway, and I was always like that — but the police made it worse, and doing what I did in the police made it much worse still'. Yet it should be remembered that he had sought the postings to the SPG, and the 'Flying Squad', and chose to walk away from the police when they wanted him to return to uniformed policing — as he put it, to 'wear a silly hat'.

Ironically — an issue rarely brought up in the secondary literature on 'cop culture' — almost all of the interviewees had stated that one of the reasons that they had joined the police was for 'security' or 'the pension'. This was not necessarily related to the money that they received, and indeed several of the interviewees had taken a drop in salary when they had accepted the job. The former detective inspector was no exception. He stated that he had joined because 'basically it was a secure job — you got a pension. I'm not going to sit here and say it was to serve the community — that's crap. It was security, and an air of power and respect . . . it certainly wasn't the money. I took a drop in salary from being a Tube driver'. However, when it was put to this interviewee that he had left the police without a pension — he had resigned rather than go back into uniform — and that his family had disintegrated around him, he still maintained that he had 'no regrets, not really. My regret is that the police changed. If it hadn't I would still be in the police, and possibly at a reasonable rank'. Thus the responsibility for his decisions and his difficulties — the fact that he would not receive his pension early, and that his family had left him — are 'the police's', rather than his own, views which can partly be understood by remembering that cynicism has long been described as a feature of cop culture.

Cynicism

One officer of six years' service said that his cynicism 'started the day I joined'. He felt that he had been held back for 12 months 'so I could be paid a lower wage', given that by that stage changes to pay and conditions meant that he would be worse off than if he had been allowed to join immediately after he had been accepted. 'The cynical side of me would say that they'd deliberately held me back to pay me a lower wage with fewer privileges.' However, this cynicism had as much to do with police work as with the pay and conditions he received: 'I put everything into each crime — each burglary, each car theft. It was almost obsessive. Then I realised it was a tide that could never be kept at bay, and so the futility comes to take over. If you do a shit job as opposed to a good job the results are still the same.' Perhaps it would be fairer to describe this as disillusionment rather than cynicism, and Howard Groves amplifies this theme a little further when he observes that police officers have a difficult job to do at the best of times, and the only time we come into contact with the public is when something goes wrong. They want to know why haven't you got the person who's done this or that to their house or car. The suspect who gets arrested claims that he's been harassed, or his family thinks that. So no one really wants to support the police.

We suspect that all of this makes the idea that policing is a 'mission' harder to sustain, especially if those people the police are supposed to be protecting fail to recognise the good that they are doing. Indeed, Howard Groves asked his student audience: 'When was the last time you went up to a policeman and just said "Hello"?' No one answered.

Partly this reflects the isolation of most police from the wider public. One interviewee described the police as being 'our own society. We have very few friends outside of the job, as the job becomes all consuming. The sense of isolation from other people because of what you do is huge. That drives the police even more inwards for their relationships and friendships'. This solidarity was reflected in the number of times the interviewees described the importance of being 'with the lads'. This was just as much a theme of the two female interviewees, although they described 'having a laugh' and 'just going out to unwind — you know socialise with each other' as the basis for their working culture. The former detective inspector was more cynical, and commented that 'what you think are friendships, they're not. They're acquaintances. Although you are part of a team, this "big family", it's shallow and false. Once the bubble looks set to burst you realise that there's nothing to it'.

One unexpected feature of 'cop culture' that emerged from this group of interviewees was a willingness to describe drug taking within their circle of colleagues. While there is no intention of suggesting that these interviews are representative of police culture as a whole, they do at the very least suggest that there are more elements of 'cop culture' to be discovered. The drug mentioned most prominently was cannabis. One male officer stated that 'smoking [cannabis] is a sub-culture. I know of six to ten individuals, and suspect a lot more smoke. I know that because I'm part of the scene — it's like a little secret society'. There were various ethical issues and practical difficulties with learning more about this secret society, but over time it was possible to uncover some of the 'glue' that kept the society together. Principally, this concerned a common interest in music — especially dance music — and not surprisingly many of those in this secret society were relatively young and not long-serving. Their relative youth and lack of experience within the service also meant that they still seemed to have significant numbers of friends outside of the police. It is perhaps of note that those within this society who did open up, were also the most willing to describe their desire to leave the police. Indeed we detected a sense of these officers 'passing through' the police — of using the force not as a career opportunity but as simply 'a job' which they would eventually change.

In short their loyalties were often compromised between — as one put it — 'their friends or the force'.

One officer described, for example, how he had briefed his friends should they be arrested. This is of note for two reasons. First, it reveals that at the very least this officer had been able to make friends outside of the circle of police colleagues, suggesting that 'solidarity' was not all-encompassing; and, secondly — and perhaps of greater academic interest — that he was prepared to collude with these friends to avoid detection and arrest. He commented that:

> I have briefed my friends about what to do if they are brought into the station on a charge — what the police would be looking for, what to say, and what not to say. For example simple possession is treated more tolerantly than intention to supply, so I try to educate my friends to have very few pills on them. Failing that, to hide them where basic stop and search procedures won't be able to go, like under the scrotum. I've tried to tell them never to keep pills in their houses, but if they have lockers at work to hide them there, or at their mum's house. At worst, to hide them in their gardens.

However, he suggested that those who took drugs were not simply friends outside of the police but included police colleagues of a variety of ranks, and 'in different kinds of jobs — uniform, traffic and detectives'. When pushed about how one entered this 'little circle', as he described it, he explained that he had been introduced to rave culture by a police colleague with whom he had shared a house: 'We used to escape down to Bournemouth for the drugs and the music. It's a subtle process based on reputation and suspicion. Usually you'll go away on a stag weekend or something like that, and one bloke would start smoking and you'd realise that lots were at it.'

It is very difficult to triangulate this information, and it took one of the authors many months of research to become sufficiently trusted to be able to report what has just been described. Nonetheless, recently on a more regular basis, our broadsheet newspapers have begun to report once again about 'corruption' within the police. A recent edition of the *Independent* (30 April 2001) for example, reported that Bill Hughes, the Director General of the National Crime Squad had had to expel 61 detectives as part of a concerted campaign to clean up the organisation. Of note, especially in relation to the interviews quoted above, Hughes explained his actions by describing that 'we have those who succumb to bribery and drug taking and drug trafficking'.

Saying and doing?

One particular objective of these interviews was to discuss the issue raised by Waddington as to whether 'saying' was related to 'doing'. In other words, whether discussions in the canteen and elsewhere actually became the basis for operational action in the streets. All of the interviewees found this a rather amusing question, believing that it was 'naive' to imagine that it was not. For example, when asked if there was a relationship between saying and doing, one male interviewee of six years' service simply replied 'Oh Hell yes'. While he accepted that some of the racism and sexism would be 'more subtle', he stated that 'they can't fight against who they are and the values that they hold. They subdue the values a little, but in times of stress and high anxiety it comes out'. Another asked, 'why do you think we have nicknames like "Action Man" or "Short Fuse"? That isn't to do with how they behave in the canteen, but how they behave in the streets'. This interviewee was adamant that 'canteen talk is street action'. The observation that the police 'can't fight against who they are and the values that they hold' rather demands the question: What are the values that the police hold? The same interviewee touched on the theme of conservatism raised by Reiner and others. He explained that the police 'prospered under the Tories — owning their own homes, shares, stronger laws — and so there is a great deal of support for them. Even the newer lads, who haven't really benefited under the Tories think that they are a good thing.

Perhaps it comes from their parents, and remember very few of them have a degree'.

Some interviewees related this question of values to their initial training. At first this seemed like an odd association to make, but as one of the female interviewees described it, 'it was pure unadulterated conditioning'. When asked to explain how this conditioning operated, she described being 'marched everywhere. You weren't allowed to be seen without a helmet . . . everything was very indoctrinated and stifling. You weren't allowed to be a person'. Howard Groves took this one stage after training by describing the first two years of a police officer's career as 'one of ostracism. New recruits are treated as "sprogs" — go make the tea, and are sent off on wild goose chases. But from the moment that they get to their two years in service, it's over. It's a form of initiation. It doesn't make it right, but it is what happens'. The end result of all this training, conditioning and ostracism — according to one interviewee — was 'think of a word that encompasses loyalty, describes when people who feel excluded come together to form a collective, to get at the people they think are against them. That's it, that's what I think police culture is'.

CONCLUSION

Our analysis of 'cop culture' provides an insight, via interviews with serving and ex-police officers, into a world too often closed to the public at large. Our sample is small, and we make no claim that it is representative, but we believe that the points that are raised illustrate some of the complexities and contradictions of the police world.

However, perhaps we should not take such forcefully expressed views at face value; after all, all nicknames like 'Action Man' and 'Short Fuse' are behavioural descriptions rather than indications of attitude or culture and, as we have emphasised elsewhere in this chapter, attitudes are not necessarily expressed in action within an operational context. That should not imply that the type of person described as having a short fuse should find a comfortable home in the police service; clearly it is an indication of a potentially dangerous characteristic. But we should be careful before assuming negative results to all aspects of police culture.

The police are not the only organisation to have a distinctive culture. Indeed, we can find elements of cynicism, conservatism, suspicion, prejudice, pragmatism and a sense of mission in many, if not most, professions. Our emphasis is not to stigmatise and criticise the police, merely to raise understanding and to emphasise the need for vigilance.

8 Private Policing and Vigilantism

INTRODUCTION

> I don't get out now and there's hardly anyone I know living in this street. I get peace of mind. Household Security comes round, and when you're living on your own and you have their phone number, it gives you peace of mind.

So says an elderly lady in Doncaster, whom we interviewed about why she paid £1 per week to an ex-offender who had set up a 'private policing' business. Her comments — and the others we gathered in researching this chapter — reveal a fundamental problem for the police: how do they respond to an increasing number of private security firms, who all claim (and some demonstrate) that they are just as, if not more, effective at keeping the peace? Should the police welcome this competition and try to incorporate these firms through training and regulation into their own culture, or should they instead attempt to close them down as unwelcome intruders who bring with them the whiff of vigilantism?

This chapter is an extended case study of a private security firm called Household Security (*cf.* Sharp and Wilson, 2000), which at its height in 1996 had a series of private foot patrols, employed 11 staff, deployed a fleet of six vans operating in Doncaster, and developed plans to extend into Milton Keynes. It continues to operate, but at a much reduced level, partly as a consequence of concerted police pressure to discredit the founder of the firm. That was not difficult to do. Malcolm Tetley (MT) is an ex-offender with a record of violence, and is a street fighter turned boxer, who spent several years in a variety of prisons prior to becoming a Jehovah's Witness and businessman. His relations with the South Yorkshire police were — and remain — difficult. In this difficulty we can see the problems posed to the police — the formal agents of household security — by private security firms who are able to respond quickly to popular anxieties about crime, and appear to offer solutions. The accommodation of Household Security by the South Yorkshire police (or lack of it) reveals much about the emergence of a strategy to be adopted by other police forces on how to deal with private security firms at a time of reduced budgets but a growing public concern about crime.

With the exception of two early Northern Irish empirical studies (Nicholas, Barr and Mollan, 1993; Thompson and Mulholland, 1994), there has been limited research into vigilantism in the UK. Johnston (1996) was the first to establish a criminological definition of 'vigilantism', and argued that it had six essential features:

(a) it involves planning and premedication by those engaging in it;
(b) its participants are private citizens whose engagement is voluntary;
(c) it is a form of 'autonomous citizenship';
(d) it uses or threatens to use force;
(e) it arises when an established order is under threat from the transgression, or potential transgression, of institutionalised norms; and
(f) it aims to control crime by offering assurances of security.

In relation to (b) above — that only private agents can undertake vigilantism — Johnston attempted to clarify the relationship between vigilantism and private security guards, even at the 'cowboy end of the market'. In doing so he rejected the idea that private security guards are vigilantist on two grounds. First, because 'it is significant that a number of police forces have already discussed the prospect of setting up their own private companies to sell police patrol services', which implies legitimisation of what private security firms do; and, secondly, despite their private status, 'commercial security companies still function within the legal ambit of the state', thus making for Johnston a distinction between *commercial* and *voluntary* activity. For Johnston the critical question was 'whether the state recognises and authorises such activity', although he did not indicate how his definition would alter if the state did not recognise or authorise the activities of a private security firm (Johnston, 1996, at 225). In relation to Household Security, very much at the 'cowboy end of the market', we will argue that these two grounds do not apply, precisely because the state, in the form of the police, refused to legitimise the activities of the firm; neither was it possible to discover whether or not 'commercial contractual law' was in fact being followed.

In the case of Household Security, it is our contention that private policing and vigilantism should be seen as being more connected than Johnston's definition allows, as a result of several unique features that are at the heart of this case study. We have already alluded to, for example, the personal history of MT as an ex-offender. Yet while many private security firms might employ, either knowingly or otherwise, ex-offenders, in the case of Household Security this fact was promoted as a positive good. In short, it became almost a marketing device — a reality commented upon favourably by clients of the firm, and a major reason why they chose to join the scheme. Secondly, the relationship between Household Security and the local police was never positive, and so the firm constantly denied a sense of being accepted or legitimised. Lastly, one of the later characteristics of the firm was informally to sub-divide, or 'franchise', the business into smaller and smaller patrols. Thus the culture of the commercial aspects of the business remained at a micro level, rooted in the individual prepared to take on the work of the patrol, and in relation to a commercial association with MT himself, rather than with the customers of the business. Indeed, we remain uncertain as to the financial arrangements of the business. This is not to imply any dishonesty, as we are certain that few businesses would have been willing to share financial information with researchers. However, it did mean that we were unable to determine whether or not, as Johnston indicates, Household Security remained 'within the legal ambit of the state'.

Thus, in constructing this case study we have been particularly keen to broaden the knowledge base of both private security firms in operation, and how this might make us reconsider theories of vigilantism. In this respect we agree with Johnston who argues for more empirical research, with a 'pressing need for the collection of basic data on the subject' (Johnston, 1996, at 234). So our focus has been on how

Household Security went about establishing its business; how it was organised; who bought its services and how these were maintained; and its relationship with the local police. This involved winning the trust of MT, and interviewing him over a period of time in Doncaster. This was not easy to do, yet there were boundaries to this trust-building process that had to be maintained so as to preserve detachment. Similarly, we interviewed at length one of his 'canvassers' who is responsible for generating business and collecting money, and went with him on his rounds. This in turn allowed us to identify customers of the business, and approach them with a view to their being interviewed as part of the research — something which Household Security was reluctant to agree to, and who attempted carefully to select those houses into which we would be allowed.

In all of this we were struck with the similarities between our research and that of Girling, Loader and Sparks (1998) in Macclesfield, who used modes of enquiry which they described as an 'ethnography of anxiety'. This is defined as:

> An analysis of publicly available information on economic, social and demographic change within the town, and of patterns of crime and demands for policing; an analysis of local representations of crime-related matters as contained in the local press and crime prevention literature; a series of focus group discussions with different sections of the local population; individual and group discussions with criminal justice professionals and other local interest groups and 'opinion formers'; a small number of biographical interviews; and numerous hours devoted to informal conversations and observation, attending meetings, hanging round police stations and travelling in police cars. (Girling, Loader and Sparks, 1998, at 389)

While our interests were more focused than this, we benefited from discussions with police officers who were familiar with Household Security — something about which MT was suspicious — and from an extensive search of local newspapers such as *The Doncaster Free Press, The Doncaster Star* and *The Milton Keynes Citizen*, all of which covered stories about the business. Similarly, we had access to all Household Security's files, which included business plans, personal and official correspondence, and advertising materials. As we continued our research, and MT's trust in us grew, he also made more personal detail available to us in the form of some 20 pages of autobiography, which he had started but had been unable to finish. However, we remained unclear as to the level of income generated, and were not given access to any formal documentation relating to the financial position of the business, or any contracts signed by the business or its customers.

In doing all of this, we could not separate Household Security from a detailed understanding of the level of crime within Doncaster, and in particular Balby where the firm is based, and of the sense of insecurity experienced by people living within the town. In constructing this picture we had access not only to official documentation made available to us by the police, but also our own understanding of this through conversation and observation based on our knowledge of the place.

Our primary method of conducting the research was by interview. As May (1993) has maintained, 'interviews yield rich insights into people's experiences, opinions, aspirations, attitudes and feelings'. We conducted a series of focused interviews with MT in the hope of allowing him the freedom to express in his own way the nature of his business, how he accounted for the business's initial success and how subsequent plans were frustrated. The focused interview is a process of building and then maintaining trust and cooperation. This was not always easy to do given the nature of MT's background, and our own, and the need to triangulate the information which he provided through discussion with others, or research with documentary sources. However, we were encouraged by Spradley's (1979) observation that the establishment of rapport in a focused interview is a four-stage process, the final stage of which is participation. During this stage the informant takes on a more assertive role and brings information to the attention of the researcher about the culture, or circumstances, under investigation. We believe that this participatory stage was reached and maintained, as is evidenced by MT's willingness to bring to us his unfinished autobiography and his request that we should complete it for him.

BALBY, HEXTHORPE AND DONCASTER

The two villages of Balby and Hexthorpe have been linked together for much of their history. In 1831, Balby-with-Hexthorpe was described as 'two pleasant villages forming a township of 420 inhabitants' (Tuffrey,

1996). The villages grew over the decades, reflecting the development of Doncaster as a railway town, and were themselves served by trams from the early 1900s. Both the villages were absorbed into Doncaster Borough in 1914, and Balby Road became the main western route for traffic from Doncaster. Balby was noted for the Pegler Brass Factory, located in Belmont Avenue, and the Springwell Lane Workhouse, which opened in 1900.

Winifred Renshaw, a former Balby resident, recalls what life in the area was like after the First World War:

Perhaps we saw more tramps because the workhouse was in Balby . . . quite often a man — or just occasionally a woman — would walk into the middle of our street [Furnival Road] and 'burst off' as mum put it, in other words start singing, walking slowly the length of our street. This was an acceptable form of begging. (Renshaw, 1984)

This same resident paints an evocative picture of the street in which she lived as a 'long row of small houses which fronted on to the street with no garden'. She also mentions that the front door opened straight into the sitting room, 'which had another door at the far side leading to the living-kitchen. Between the two rooms a flight of steep dark stairs led up to the bedrooms' (Renshaw, 1984). While much has changed with the housing stock of this area, there is a sense of continuity that this description captures. Kevin Keegan, for example, who moved to 36 Waverley Avenue in Balby in the late 1950s and was to work at Pegler's Brass Factory, remembers that 'the back garden was pretty small', but was still delighted that at least he had an inside toilet and electric light (Keegan, 1997, at 47). Mrs Renshaw also provides a rather nostalgic picture of law and order:

We were I think a law-abiding lot, but we had a healthy respect for authority and when the word went round 'Bobby's coming' we made sure we were engaged in our most innocent pursuits, guaranteed not to cause damage or annoy the residents. We knew that no transgression would escape the policeman's eye and if he caught us up to mischief he would haul us off to our parents where we would get short shrift. (Renshaw, 1984)

This memory of law and order may or may not be accurate, but perhaps it establishes an historic ideal against which to measure present realities.

Indeed Balby has fallen on hard times, a process which seems to have started with the road widening scheme of Balby Road in the early 1960s, which carved Balby into at least two distinct parts, and which coincided with the decline of industry and enterprise in the area. Even the workhouse was to close in 1974. As a result, by 1989, 12 per cent of the population of Balby were unemployed. This emerging pattern within Balby might also explain a 1.4 per cent decrease in population between 1981 and 1991, from 14,528 people to 14,325. It is also significant that Balby has one of the highest percentages of people living in the area who are over the age of 75, and almost 20 per cent of the population are of pensionable age. Nonetheless, the sense of homogeneity alluded to by Winifred Renshaw remains, at least in relation to ethnicity, and (again using figures from the 1991 census) only 2.5 per cent of the population comprise people from ethnic minorities. All of this is mirrored in Doncaster's own fortunes. Between 1971 and 1984 there were 6,000 job losses in manufacturing, and a spate of colliery and factory closures. Not surprisingly, unemployment remains high, and is consistently above the British average (Doncaster Metropolitan Borough Council, 1990).

CRIME AND THE SOUTH YORKSHIRE POLICE

The South Yorkshire police's 'A' Divisional Crime Profile for 1992 provides the most recent formal picture of crime in Doncaster. This document is clearly not a neutral source, neither does it tell us anything about the actual crime levels of the area, only about those crimes that are reported by the public. Nonetheless, it is of use within this context in that, by revealing a pattern of reported criminal activity, it provides a backdrop against which to place both Household Security and the response to the company by the South Yorkshire police. After all, Household Security has to be able to offer a service which people want, or feel that they need, and the figures supplied by the police reveal something of the context within which the company operated.

The Doncaster 'A' Division incorporates the geographic borough of Doncaster and is divided into three sub-divisions: Doncaster Town (A1); Thorne (A2); and Mexborough (A3). The A1 sub-division contains the town centre, Balby, Hexthorpe, Hyde Park, Town Moor, Wheatley, Intake, and Cantley and Bessacarr. Overall, A Division experienced an

increase of reported crime of 34.44 per cent between 1987 and 1991.
The highest reported increases over the five years related to house
burglary, up by 52.48 per cent; burglary from premises other than
dwellings, up by 86.5 per cent; and theft of, and from, cars, both of
which were up by over 60 per cent. (See Table 8.1 below.)

Offence	1987	1991	Increase (%)
Burglary/dwelling	2,058	3,138	52.48
Burglary/premises other than dwelling	2,526	4,711	86.50
Theft and taking of vehicle	1,727	2,842	64.56
Theft from unattended vehicle	2,721	4,525	66.30

Source: Doncaster 'A' Divisional Crime Profile 1992

Table 8.1   Reported crime A Division Doncaster 1987–1991

It is important to consider this general profile against those of the
three sub-divisions. The A1 division, for example, which incorporates
Balby, experienced an overall increase in reported crime of 34.75 per
cent, slightly higher than the general overall increase experienced by the
whole division. Specific areas within the A1 sub-division had unique
problems, which is not surprising given that the A1 sub-division
contains the town centre, which has over 40 public houses and four
night-clubs. Balby is also seen as having distinct policing problems, and
is described in the crime profile as 'consisting mainly of the older type
terraced property, which are an easy target for the criminal resulting in
a higher incidence of burglary offences in the area' (Doncaster 'A'
Division Crime Profile, 1992, at 20). Indeed, there were 4,387 domestic
burglaries in the A1 sub-division between 1987 and 1991, of which the
Crime Profile claims some 41 per cent were detected. Whether this
detection rate is accurate or not, the problem of domestic burglary
within the sub-division can be gauged by comparing the five most often
reported crimes in 1987 with those reported in 1991. As can be seen in
Table 8.2 below, domestic burglary did not feature as one of the five
most commonly reported crimes in 1987, but by 1991 it accounted for
just under 12 per cent of all crimes reported to the police within the
sub-division. This is further underscored by the fact that the number of

domestic burglaries reported to the police doubled between 1987 and 1991, from 680 in 1987 to 1,353 in 1991, an increase of some 98 per cent.

Offence	1987 — % of total reported crime	Offence	1991 — % of total reported crime
Shoplifting	16.8	Theft from vehicle	19.1
Theft from vehicle	14.6	Burglary other premises	11.9
Burglary other premises	9.7	Burglary dwellings	11.8
TWLA	9.48	Shoplifting	11.2
Criminal damage	9.19	Criminal damage	10.9

Source: Doncaster 'A' Division Crime Profile 1992

Table 8.2   Most commonly reported crimes 1987–1991

In a series of revealing passages, the anonymous author of the Crime Profile attempts to explain why these increases occurred and offer 'the way forward'. The author suggests, for example, that three factors partly account for the overall increase in the level of reported crime. These are a 'greater concern in communities where members of the public now want to report a crime which previously they were reluctant to do', 'insurance consciousness', and 'monetary gain through the Criminal Injuries Compensation Board' (Doncaster 'A' Divisional Crime Profile, at 1992, at 25). The author is also keen to establish that young people in particular are likely to be at the heart of the cause of this increase in the rate of reported crime, and suggests that some 75 per cent of crime committed in the division is the responsibility of 15–21-year-olds. This observation also forms the basis of the author's 'way forward', in that it is suggested that 'the possibility and benefit of police officers seconded full-time to schools to become a normal part of the school scene must not be discounted ... the expansion of police officers into schools as part of the teaching staff must be seen as a positive way forward into the 21st century' (Doncaster 'A' Divisional Crime Profile, 1992, at 76).

Greater schools liaison, with full-time police staff members, is not the only suggestion within the 'way forward'. The author also suggests video surveillance, better crime prevention initiatives related to cars, and the end of 'overcrowding in licensed premises and the supply of gimmicky cocktails'. However, the author is also at pains to point out that 'there can be no doubt that crime will continue to rise annually', and as such 'the police service cannot be expected to shoulder the burden of crime alone'. Everyone in 'the fight against crime ... must play his or her part', which meant that

> The involvement of the public whether in groups or individually can only be a good thing ... The way forward by the police service will be to encourage innovative schemes and ideas and the assistance and advice of outside agencies, to reduce the levels of crime and the public's perception of the fear of crime. (Doncaster 'A' Divisional Crime Profile, 1992, at 76–77)

THE ORIGINS OF HOUSEHOLD SECURITY

As the philosophy of Household Security is so interwoven with the personal philosophy of MT, some attempt will be made to provide personal detail where this is appropriate, as well as a description of how the business worked in practice. In short, to provide an explanation of the 'culture' of the business, of MT, and of his employees.

Household Security began operating in Balby in September 1993. The origins of the idea are confused, but seem to stem both from MT's personal history — his dislike of bullies who plagued him at school because of a childhood stutter, and his background as a street-fighter, doorman and boxer — and the identification of a business opportunity. This business idea may have come from John Rushton, a boxing promoter with whom MT had worked and who had originally encouraged MT to go into crowd control. However, MT claims that instead of this 'I wanted to go into patrolling ... well, because I saw the burglaries that were happening in the area'. Thus he takes the police author of the Crime Profile at his word, in that he comes up with an innovative scheme to reduce the levels of crime being experienced by the area. As preparation for the business, MT conducted a street survey of St Peter's Road, Balby — where he himself lived — and discovered that there was almost universal support for the idea of a street patrol. In August 1993, just a month before the business got off the ground, *The*

Doncaster Star described the interest in the business, and interviewed several residents of St Peter's Road: 'Almost all the residents of St Peter's Road, weary of the constant attacks which see their homes burgled, their cars broken into, and even their garden sheds stripped, have signed up.'

Ironically, MT's autobiography provides some history of his and his family's relationship with St Peter's Road:

> We were thorough villains — everybody in the neighbourhood knew us, nothing was safe. At twelve years old my brother Paul would start at the end of St Peter's Road, a street in Balby consisting of eighty or ninety houses, finding out if anyone was in their homes. A lot of people used to be out. He would do one house at a time breaking in and robbing the gas meters. By the time three or four hours had lapsed, he would carry a bag of shillings.

Nonetheless, it was this and other local streets that MT and Household Security now set out to protect; and fortified by the local publicity and MT's surveying of the area, the firm started to offer a security service. This service had various components, which evolved and were described in different ways, partly in response to local interest and police criticism. However, in essence what MT provided was a night-time foot patrol of those houses that joined the scheme at a cost of £1 per week. Houses joining the scheme placed a sticker in their windows, which read 'WARNING! THESE PREMISES PATROLLED BY HOUSEHOLD SECURITY', and the foot patrols shone a light on the windows of those houses in the scheme to show that they had been checked, and presumably to provide reassurance to the occupants. MT described the patrol aspect of the business as follows:

> We have a van with a driver and two guards on foot ... It was just a night patrol. Really all I wanted to give was peace of mind. The peace of mind was a sticker ... the van goes round at night-time to the customers we've got. There's two guards in the van shining lamps on the houses and round the back ... we're a deterrent.

However, it is the nature of this 'deterrence' which is of interest. MT described it in newspaper interviews that he gave as follows:

The principle is simple: if you put a scarecrow in a field, the crows don't come anywhere near. It's the same with security. Our uniformed officers maintain a visible presence. No burglar in his right mind would think of working in an area we cover. (*The Doncaster Courier*, 17 June 1994)

MT continued this 'scarecrow' theme in interview, describing it as 'common-sense', and maintaining that 'if there's no policemen there, the crows are at it ... all it's down to is being visible in the situation'. Yet some 'scarecrows' work better than others, and MT seems to be acknowledging this in the last sentence of his interview with *The Doncaster Courier*. Household Security is a better scarecrow for, as MT accepts during interviews with us, 'there's only one person who can do this job and that's a villain ... they have great respect for that person in these areas, and the people in the housing estates will know this, and they will be left alone'.

Inevitably this raises the issue of MT's own history of violence, both as a street fighter, doorman and boxer, and as an offender who served time for, amongst other things assaulting a policeman. To what extent does Household Security reflect this violence, or potential for violence? (It should also be noted that the use of violence, or the threat to use violence, is one of Johnston's definitions of 'vigilantism'.) In newspaper interviews which he gave, MT described the business as 'non violent' (see *The Doncaster Courier*, 17 June 1994 and *The Milton Keynes Citizen*, 7 November 1996). In interview with us, MT talked about the 'respect' that he was given within the local area, which does not necessarily equate with violence but might reflect a potential for violence. When asked to describe why this respect was given, for example, MT found it easier to relate the concept back to his time in prison:

The only way that I can explain it to you is if I'm in prison and I'm Jack the Lad, nobody will mess about or they'll get some of that. So, they respect that. The motives might not be right — I want some respect here so don't mess. So you give somebody a good slap on t'arse with a cane, and they won't do it again. That's the answer. That is the only answer ... there's some nasty people out there that want done. They want sorting out, don't they? We live in a system where the fist matters.

Indeed, MT acknowledged that on one occasion that he had had to 'have a word with one Jack the Lad and told him to leave the stickers alone in that area', although this is the only specific example that he provided during interview. Nevertheless, his reputation was well known, and would surely also be enough to have frightened many would-be burglars off the 'sticker' houses. In fact MT saw this displacement of burglary from the poorer areas of Balby to the more middle class areas of Doncaster as one of the reasons that the police became so antagonistic towards the business (see below). MT's offending background was positively promoted as publicity for the business, and leaflets used by Household Security openly describe, MT as an 'ex-offender'. Similarly, when MT recruited people as foot patrols, while he refused to take on anyone with a history of burglary, 'if they had a record of violence I'd set them on'. However, he was quick to add, 'not that I wanted them to knock people about — it wasn't like that'.

Whether it was 'like that' or not, the business grew rapidly. Perhaps understandably, MT was reluctant to go into great detail about the number of houses he guarded, as this would reveal the amount of income that he generated, but he did provide some information. For example, in taking the decision to franchise the business he described having at that time — early 1996 — '3,000 customers, so that's £12,000 per month', although he points out that in franchising the business he only got a 'fraction of that'. Nonetheless, by this stage he had also expanded the business to guarding building sites, and in 'the first 10 months we did £80,000 worth of business'. He consistently maintained that the business 'got too big'. As such:

> I thought 'well, it's too big so I must think ahead'. So I split the guards who worked for me and gave them areas and said that they had to look after them. I told them to put stickers in the windows, and that I would take a percentage of what came back each month ... I did it as a franchise because I saw that it was too big for one person to collect.

Despite our best efforts we were unable to interview or observe any of the franchisees; but given that the business was very publicly associated with MT himself, it is perhaps safe to assume that they were not as successful and had fallen by the wayside. Indeed, one of the canvassers we interviewed (see below) might provide another explanation for franchisees failing to prosper: '... people got fed up working seven days a week — it was a hard job'. Nonetheless, it is clear that Household Security had indeed tapped into a local feeling of insecurity and disenchantment with the formal agents of policing, and that MT's offending history, far from putting people off the business, had become a positive boon.

THE CUSTOMERS OF HOUSEHOLD SECURITY

As has been described above, our requests to interview customers of the business were almost always refused. Neither did we feel able simply to identify customers independently of MT as this fact would have been relayed back to him very quickly, destroying any trust that we had built up. Nonetheless, we were able to interview customers when we accompanied Robin Eldridge (RE) as he went on his weekly rounds to collect money. We also interviewed RE at length, given that he had been employed by the business almost since its beginnings and in a variety of roles. Initially, for example, he had been employed as a 'canvasser' — knocking on people's doors to offer the security service — but his job was now to collect money. He also advised us that he had gone on foot patrol, although it should be pointed out that RE is in his seventies. In accompanying RE were we able not only to observe the business in operation, but also to listen to conversations between RE and the customers about crime that took place. We had to be introduced to those customers, and, despite our best efforts, RE insisted on describing us as 'academics', which seemed to impart a certain gravitas to the proceedings. On the other hand, this description did facilitate access.

The interviews were unplanned — the customers interviewed were chosen on a random basis depending on who happened to be home when RE knocked on the door. We do not pretend that these customers are in any way representative of the business's customers, as we were never given access to any database — if this existed — from which to choose a representative sample. All the interviewees were taped in their homes with their permission, and promised anonymity. Inevitably the interviews were based on a hastily assembled semi-structure, and lasted on average 30 minutes. This time scale is of relevance given that RE was actually attempting to collect money from a variety of customers and that he refused to allow us to continue discussion with the customers by ourselves. Thus we could ask only as many questions as we felt able without jeopardising RE's support for the interviews. Some general characteristics of the interviewees can be provided. In all, eight customers were interviewed. This is undoubtedly a small sample, but nonetheless offers valuable insight into the hopes and fears of the customers of the business. All except one was an owner-occupier, and they lived in King Edward Road, Westfield Road or Littlemore Lane. Four of the interviewees were female, four male, and all were white. Their average ages were 64 for the women, and 63 for the men; the youngest person interviewed was a woman aged 53, and the oldest a woman aged 85. This is not so dissimilar to the age profile of the area, where people of pensionable age make up some 20 per cent of the residents, and which is almost overwhelmingly white. Most had been with Household Security for five years and thus can be regarded as 'satisfied customers'. The interviews were planned as much as possible around a series of four question areas: (i) the customer's personal experience of crime; (ii) the type of service provided by Household Security; (iii) why they chose to use Household Security rather than the police; and (iv) their knowledge of MT's background. Of note, in discussing these areas with customers of the business, we were also able, albeit in a small way, to test further Johnston's definition of 'vigilantism', most obviously in relation to what the customers perceived was at the heart of the service they bought. This is no small matter, for it became clear that one of the reasons that these customers had employed Household Security was because the firm was perceived as working outside of contractual and other laws, and as such could use tactics which were denied to the police. In particular they identified that Household Security would be prepared to use force to deal with burglars, or (as one customer put it), to 'wave a big stick'.

EXPERIENCES OF CRIME

Despite being long-established customers of the business, no one interviewed had any direct experience of crime. Three customers mentioned that they had had trouble with people parking in the streets late at night, and all described burglaries that had taken place in the area, but in a general way. So, for example, burglaries took place 'across the road', or at 'the other end of Balby'. Information about crime came from, according to Interviewee #4, a male aged 63, 'reading the newspapers — every day you could read about a burglary in Balby'. Interviewee #8, also a male aged 63, found out about crime from the local pub: '... when you go out in the evening you hear these tales'. Given this lack of direct experience of crime, most of the customers, echoing the phrase used in Household Security's promotional literature, explained that they employed the firm for 'peace of mind'. Interviewee #1, a woman aged 85 — the oldest person interviewed — provided a typical reply: 'I don't get out now, and there's hardly anyone I know living in this street. I get peace of mind. Household Security comes round, and when you're living on your own and you have their phone number, it gives you peace of mind.'

THE SERVICE OFFERED BY HOUSEHOLD SECURITY

All the interviewees mentioned this active dimension of 'coming round', which was seen by all as a difference between what Household Security was able to offer compared with the local police. Other descriptions of the service that had been bought included: 'they check the premises — check that everything is locked up'; 'they're guards'; and 'they patrol the streets'. Interviewee #6, a woman aged 53, confirmed the nature of the patrol that had been described in interview by MT: 'They patrol at night. You can see a beam of light coming through your window to show you that they're out there, and that they've come round.'

WHY PAY HOUSEHOLD SECURITY RATHER THAN USE THE POLICE?

Inevitably, descriptions of the kind above quickly led to police/ Household Security comparisons. Three themes emerged when we queried why the interviewees chose to buy a service rather than rely on the police: (i) the deterrent effect of the sticker and patrol; (ii) the pro-active nature of Household Security as opposed to the reactive nature of the police; and (iii) the fact that Household Security did not have it's 'hands tied', and so could sort out problems in very different ways to how the police would deal with crime and criminals. This last theme is clearly related to the customers' understanding of MT's background, and will be discussed more fully below.

All eight interviewees mentioned the deterrent effect of the business, although different interviewees concentrated on specific aspects of the service. Interviewee #5, for example, a woman aged 53, described the deterrent effect of having a Household Security sticker in her window: '... it's like having a burglar alarm up'. She amplified this statement by describing a burglary that had occurred at 'the other end of the road', although she could not date when this burglary took place, and why she believed that her house had not been burgled: '... our deterrent was the burglar alarm, the double glazing, and the Household Security sticker — it was easier to go somewhere else.' Similarly, Interviewee #4 described 'never having been burgled' but that neighbours had been, and put this down to Household Security: '... they seemed like something that would help keep it down — they'd deter burglary.' He also echoed the advertising theme of the business, describing the fact that Household Security gave him 'peace of mind — there's always someone at night keeping an eye on your property. I can see their vans, and their lights.'

The second theme to emerge was that Household Security was seen to be proactive in its fight against burglary, as compared with the police who were described as 'reactive'. At one level this was seen in the ability of Household Security to be available to deal with problems. Interviewee #2, for example, a man aged 68, commented favourably on the business as 'it takes time to get hold of the police'. This theme of time was taken up by Interviewee #6, who said that 'the police only come if you phone them and it might take three or four hours for them to get round to you'. Similarly, Interviewee #7, a man aged 57, commented that 'the police come after its happened, but Household Security come before its happened'. Interviewee #3, a man aged 63, felt that the police 'don't have the resources to patrol up and down ... it is difficult enough to get them to come out if you've had a burglary'.

Customers of the business saw the issue of resources as being the reason why the police could not be as effective as Household Security. Interviewee #5 mentioned the 'cuts and cuts' experienced by the police, for example, which is echoed by Interviewee #4: 'It is the police's responsibility to deter burglary, but circumstances — their finances going down. They don't have enough bobbies on the streets. When I joined Household Security you never saw a bobby up here in Balby.' Interviewee #6 thought that the police 'don't have time' as a result of their expenditure cuts, and Interviewee #8 that 'the police have got too much on their hands anyway'. This particular interviewee seemed to be indicating that he felt that his problems were too minor for the police to be bothered with, and compared this with a 'bespoke' policing service provided by Household Security: 'The police don't get as close to you as Household Security. You see their van coming round late at night, and they shine their torches. If I go away at the weekend, they'll come and check your door — front and back — and I know that that happens as the neighbours tell me.'

The last theme to emerge was the ability of the business to 'sort things out', as opposed to the police who 'have their hands tied'. Interviewee #7, for example, describes this idea most clearly: '. . . the police's hands are tied . . . they're frightened to wave the big stick. With these people [Household Security], for a very small amount of money, they'll wave that big stick.' Similarly, Interviewee #6 described how she believes Household Security (as opposed to the police) would deal with a criminal:

> If the police caught someone doing something wrong, well they'd just take them away and then release them. But criminals are actually frightened of the people running the security firm, because they know that there will be no messing about. The police can't do that. If a policeman grabbed someone by the scruff of the neck, what would happen to that policeman? He'd get accused of abusing the person who had been robbing you. I don't think that these blokes [Household Security] will have a second thought for them. They'd get them and give them a kick up their backsides and that'd be that.

Interviewee #7 put all of this more succinctly: '. . . everyone knows that if they break into a home guarded by Household Security they'll get their arses kicked. It's as simple as that.' Lastly, Interviewee #5 attempted to provide a 'common-sense' criminological perspective on all of this, commenting that 'criminals know criminals'. She continued:

> If one criminal group knows that another criminal group is protecting an area then they'll be put off going into that area. They're not so worried — the criminals — about the Law, but if they go into another criminal's patch of land, there will be repercussions if you know what I mean.

Several others of the interviewees echoed this common-sense perspective, including Interviewee #4, who felt that Household Security 'know how burglars think ... so they can advise you about locks and bolts'. All of this is clearly related to the interviewees' knowledge of MT's offending background, which we now discuss.

KNOWLEDGE OF OFFENDING HISTORY

All of the interviewees were aware of MT's criminal past, and all saw that past as a positive advantage in the business he now ran. Interviewee #3, a woman aged 63, was initially rather sensitive about addressing the subject, but then provided a series of useful observations:

> Am I supposed to say the truth? They say that's its rogues who've been in prison who run it. It's also what the police say. I don't know if it's rogues — that's the sort of thing that the police would say as they don't like people who aren't official doing their job. If it is rogues, they would know the kind of thing that criminals do. They might also know some of the people who are doing it. I also think that they'll be in the firing line from the police if something did happen to your home, and therefore they'll take good care of it, but the story being out about is that they are all iffy.

All of this related back to earlier 'common-sense' analyses of Household Security's strengths and weaknesses, although it did add a new dimension in that this woman believed that the business had more to lose if a burglary was committed in the street. The idea of 'criminals knowing criminals' described above was developed further by Interviewee #7, who maintained that he was 'not bothered' about the criminal record of MT, as he 'can do the job':

> All their life they've made their living doing this. It's not legitimate what they've done, but he has used his brain to see that he can use that knowledge and turn it into a weapon for everyone else. So when you hear some of the people Household Security is made up of, you know that people avoid them — they won't just tell them 'you're naughty lads' — they'll kick them up the arse.

Others, such as Interviewee #4, saw MT's criminal record as history — 'as far as I'm concerned he's done his time, and started again' — although the most common reaction to the fact of MT's offending history was to see this as a positive advantage. Not only did customers believe that this allowed him to understand the thinking of would-be burglars, thus being in a better position to deter them, but he was also able to deal more effectively with criminals than a cash-strapped, hard-pressed police force, which was in any event seen to be constrained from taking action.

We have already acknowledged that it is difficult to see how representative of all the business's customers these eight interviewees are, but some measure of triangulation can be provided from interviews done by various newspapers who covered the story, and through evidence provided by Household Security itself. For example, MT collected a series of petitions in support of the business, to which we were given access, and we were subsequently able to verify names and addresses on the petitions with the local phone directory. (These petitions were largely used by Household Security in its increasingly bitter attacks against the police, which is described below.) Of course not everyone who signed a petition was willing to pay for the security service, but time and again newspaper coverage of the business generated a great deal of support, much of it echoing the comments of those who were interviewed. As the business was being set up, *The Doncaster Star*, for example, interviewed people who had signed up for the patrol in St Peter's Road. Peter Powell was one of those residents interviewed by the paper. He said he had joined the scheme because 'I believe in what these people are trying to do ... this is a bad area for crime, and so I'm all for anything which will help to stop it'. Another resident, Monica Coney, stated that she had paid for the patrol as 'we're worried about the car', and Lorraine Panks had decided to buy the services of Household Security as 'it's terrible down here ... [burglaries] are happening all the time. This patrol is a good idea' (*The Doncaster Star*, 3 August 1993). The paper later covered a demonstration of supporters of the business from Balfour Road in Bentley, protesting about alleged police harassment of Household Security. Among the protestors was Christine Tinkler, Balfour Road's Neighbourhood Watch coordinator, who is quoted as saying 'I think that the street patrols are absolutely brilliant ... the police cannot compare because the money is not there ... people are not interested in

Neighbourhood Watch any more. I know that under Mr Tetley's scheme I have got peace of mind' (*The Doncaster Star*, 4 August 1994).

HOUSEHOLD SECURITY AND THE SOUTH YORKSHIRE POLICE

Relations between Household Security and the South Yorkshire police were never cordial. An increasingly bitter war of words broke out between various police spokesmen and MT in the local Doncaster press. This in turn led to MT publicly protesting outside Doncaster police headquarters, and eventually to his writing to John Major and Tony Blair, and finally making a formal complaint against the South Yorkshire police for harassment to the Police Complaints Authority (PCA). Whether this had to do with the offending history of MT, or other issues that we discuss below, it is clear that the police did not assess Household Security as a legitimate provider of private protection within the community. This is not to accept that they victimised MT, although some *prima facie* evidence to substantiate this claim exists, but rather it draws attention to the difficulties faced by police forces in how to respond to and assess private security firms who might in fact be in a much better position to provide 'peace of mind'. It also underscores for us the need to expand upon Johnston's attempt to clarify the relationship between vigilantism and private security guards.

Relations between the business and the police were difficult almost from the beginning. In the very first article in the local press that covered Household Security, Doncaster Divisional Commander Michael Thompson was quoted as saying:

> The principle behind this idea sounds great but the problem is the reaction it could have on the streets. There is a terrible danger it could lead to people taking the law into their own hands. I can appreciate why people are interested in this kind of operation but my advice would be not to get involved. (*The Doncaster Star*, 3 August 1993)

This response set out from the start a position whereby the police refused to accept that the business was legitimate — hardly an auspicious start for any company just getting going — and Commander Thompson also clearly advised people not to become involved with Household

Security. Indeed, while not directly calling the business 'vigilantist', Commander Thompson did allude to this in his observation about 'taking the law into their own hands'. This position did not materially change, although the police did raise other objections. For example, they objected to the service on the grounds of cost (see *Doncaster Free Press*, 14 July 1994); that it pandered unduly to public fears (see *The Doncaster Star*, 21 July 1994); that the competence of the foot patrols to deal with offenders was suspect (see *The Doncaster Star*, 21 July 1994); and that the firm would disperse burglary into 'poorer' areas which were not guarded by Household Security (see *The Doncaster Free Press*, 14 July 1994). Throughout this very public debate, Chief Superintendent Brian Mordew, who was in charge of 'A' Division, called for the 'legal control and regulation of these groups' (*The Doncaster Star*, 15 February 1994).

In one sense these difficulties did not seem to affect Household Security too greatly. After all, the publicity was in fact generally favourable to the business and seemed to generate much more interest in the firm, including an appearance for MT on GMTV. Indeed, as long as the debate was conducted at a public level there were distinct advantages for Household Security in allowing this to continue. Local people were becoming educated about the issues involved and thus were better able to judge who would provide a more effective service. MT proved to be quite adept at generating publicity, and seemed to be able to hold his own against Chief Superintendent Mordew, who was reduced on one occasion to claiming that he opposed the firm's 'fast response' vehicles because they 'broke the speed limits' (*The Doncaster Star*, 14 July 1994). However, what was of greater concern to MT was his belief that a less than public 'vendetta' was being conducted against him and his business at a street level, as opposed to being confined to a debate about formal policing policy and private security firms.

This vendetta, according to MT, took two forms: (i) general harassment of MT, and his staff; and (ii) the undermining or, as he put it, the 'rubbishing' of the service that he provided by rank and file police officers working within the community. We will deal with each of these issues in turn, but first it is important to acknowledge that we only had detailed access to MT and his files, which contain some, but not all, of the police correspondence on this matter. Equally, while we informally interviewed several senior police officers in Doncaster who stated that they were willing to work with Household Security, it was not necessarily officers at this level who seemed to be causing day-to-day problems. What is known for certain is that MT raised a complaint against the South Yorkshire police with the PCA in 1996, which was settled 'informally', and that at one stage he was threatening to sue the police for loss of earnings. He remains disenchanted with the South Yorkshire police, and this disenchantment might have been the motivating force behind his attempting to start up a business in Milton Keynes. (See *Milton Keynes Citizen*, 7 November 1996.)

The first incident of alleged harassment occurred in October 1993, just after the business had started, when MT was patrolling in his van at 03:45 hours. The van was pulled over by a police patrol vehicle, and according to an interview given by MT to *The Doncaster Star*:

> One of the two police officers asked me to get out of our van and said that I had been stopped because a rear brake light was not working. We checked it and it was OK. Then he asked me my name and when I said 'Malcolm' he said 'Tetley, isn't it?' — so he knew who I was, and then he issued me with a form to produce my driving documents. The van has our company name on the side. There was nothing wrong with the lights, and the police know that we are patrolling so why did this officer stop us? It smacks of harassment or even victimisation. (*The Doncaster Star*, 15 October 1993)

MT claims that his vehicles are regularly stopped and asked for certification, and we can confirm that in 1996 his vehicles were stopped at least 22 times by the police asking for MT to produce insurance and MoT documentation. There is also some evidence to suggest that Household Security vehicles are given parking tickets when they stop, thus making it difficult to fulfil their guarding function.

MT also claims that the police unofficially undermine or 'rubbish' Household Security. It is difficult to confirm this, but MT has kept copious notes of conversations that he has had with various police officers whom he has anonymously telephoned, asking for their advice about whether or not he should join Household Security. If these notes are to be believed, these officers have never supported the scheme, questioning the 'dubious characters' who run it and advising the caller to 'have nothing too do with Household Security'. This is hardly a credible source, but what is more certain is MT's annoyance at this 'harassment', which drove him to lead a public protest about his treatment outside Doncaster police headquarters in August 1994. Of note, he was accompanied on this protest by residents of Balfour Street in Bentley, Doncaster, who were by this stage being guarded by Household Security, and who were in support of the patrols.

At the conclusion of these claims, denials and counter-claims, we are left with the inescapable conclusion that the South Yorkshire police did not support Household Security either at a formal policy level, as partners in the fight against a rising reported crime rate (which had been so graphically presented in the 'A' Divisional Crime Profile of 1992), or at the level of local beat police officers working in Balby. The firm did seem to generate support from its customers, who were prepared to judge Household Security on the service that it provided rather than on the basis of cost, legitimacy, competence, or the fact that it might 'disperse' burglary to 'poorer areas'. (Indeed, on the contrary, as it is MT's belief that the police do not like his business because burglary has been dispersed to the areas where the police and 'the middle classes' live.) Undoubtedly this customer support does also stem from a belief that in employing an ex-offender they are setting 'a thief to catch a thief', and that in doing so he will be able to take extra-legal measures, denied to the police, to put a stop to crime. This belief generates for MT a substantial income, which might or might not be justified on the basis of the 'peace of mind' that is provided.

CONCLUSION

This chapter has been concerned with testing Johnston's theoretical definition of 'vigilantism'. In particular, it has sought to test the distinction he drew between private security firms — even at 'the cowboy end of the market' — and vigilantism, through a detailed analysis of one such private security firm. In doing so we would argue that the distinction drawn by Johnston between such firms and vigilante action is far less clear than he has presented, and we are unable to verify his assertion of the 'crucial' difference between private *commercial* and *voluntary* activity. Household Security may indeed have had a commercial purpose — MT wanted to make money — although it is impossible to tell how this commercial activity is regulated, if at all; but the origins, development and working culture of the business relate specifically to its perceived ability to operate outside of the 'legal ambit of the state'. That was and remains Household Security's unique selling point, and precisely why it was so successful. Customers paid their £1 per week because they believed that in doing so they had hired something different to formal models of policing, or indeed of private security firms.

9 A Vision for the Future

INTRODUCTION

General Roberto Conforti is an Italian police officer, but as he invites us into his office it becomes clear that he is no ordinary police officer. Around the walls are beautiful paintings, and every available space is covered in Apulian antiquities. As the Head of the *Comando Carabinieri Tutela Patrimonio Artistico* in Rome, General Conforti is charged with recovering stolen and looted antiquities, and so successful has he been that he shows us several beautiful, bound guidebooks of all the treasures that he and his team have retrieved — some of which are openly on display. After exchanging pleasantries, we wander into the main offices of the *Comando Carabinieri*, where seemingly scores of police officers scurry around looking at the sales catalogues of art and auction houses from around the World, in the hope of matching something which has been stolen with property that has been put up for sale.

To help them with this task, General Conforti has invested heavily in computer technology, and as we wait for the General one of his staff switches on his computer and shows us a map which traces the route that stolen Italian antiquities are believed to follow. First the stolen goods go to Switzerland where, we are advised, they acquire a provenance — seemingly what usually becomes known as 'the property of a gentleman' — and thereafter they are sold to England, Germany, the United States or Japan. By the time the General returns, a computer link has been established with two police officers in another Italian city to discuss a recent theft by the *tombaroli* — the tomb robbers — who are at the bottom of this particular illegal hierarchy, and subsequent links are made with police forces in Holland and France. We ask about liaison with British police, and while the General is politeness personified, it becomes clear that the British still do not have the computer technology to create a link to Rome.

This visit confirmed for us a major theme that we would wish to expand upon in this chapter. Put simply, whether we like it or not, the future of policing in this country is intimately bound up with the future of policing in Europe and beyond. Crime does not respect national borders, and inevitably many of the crime problems in Britain have started as criminal opportunities elsewhere, which in turn can only be controlled by greater European police cooperation. So while we began this chapter by looking at the illegal trade in antiquities — not necessarily a crime which is high on the Government's agenda — if we had chosen to focus on, for example, drugs, we could have described how the single market which has flowed from greater European unification and freedom of movement has in effect also created a single market in crime. This reality needs to prompt our police to become far more outward-looking in their approach to crime, which in turn will have a major impact on virtually everything that they do — from the need for greater language training, to prompting greater liaison with Europol.

A SINGLE MARKET IN CRIME

European cooperation between police, customs and judicial authorities takes place within the European Union (EU) under the banner of 'justice and home affairs' (JHA), and JHA already accounts for a third of all paperwork passing through British permanent representation in Brussels (Hall, 1999, at 1). JHA encompasses two different sets of issues: (i) migration, and (ii) the fight against organised international crime. The first attempt to coordinate EU policy on JHA was made at Maastricht in 1991, and a variety of other treaties and agreements have had to be established to facilitate this growing cooperation, including the Schengen Agreement in 1990, which led in 1995 to the removal of internal passport controls within the EU, a fact incorporated within the EU's legal framework by the 1997 Treaty of Amsterdam. Hall (1999, at 5) sees this freedom of movement and travel within the EU as creating greater criminal opportunities. Freedom of movement within Europe in turn puts additional pressure on those countries seeking full membership of the EU, as their membership inevitably expands the EU's borders still further. Thus Greece, which borders Albania, Macedonia, Turkey and Bulgaria, will have to establish better frontier controls, for once she gains full membership and benefits from the Schengen Agreement, anyone who enters Greece will have unlimited freedom of movement throughout the EU.

The linkage of migration, immigration and crime is, of course, a controversial one. After all, they do not necessarily go hand in hand. However, at a more practical policing level, the Schengen Agreement also allowed for the 'hot pursuit' of suspects from one member state to another, so that in effect police in pursuit of someone suspected of committing a crime, or an offender who has escaped custody, may follow into a neighbouring member state where they are allowed to catch or detain the suspect. Thus police in Kent could legitimately pursue a suspect through the Channel Tunnel on Eurostar, and detain that suspect on French territory. However, Schengen's greatest contribution to better law enforcement cooperation has been the Schengen Information System (SIS), which has a central secretariat in Strasbourg. This is a network of national criminal databases which contains information on, for example, stolen vehicles and people sought for extradition or suspected of having committed serious offences. By 1997 it contained 14 million records, and member states posted 5.5 million alerts in that year alone (Hall, 1999, at 30).

While the SIS seems to have become quickly accepted as a policing tool, Europol has served a much longer apprenticeship. Europol — which should not be confused with Interpol — was established by the Maastricht Treaty and is based in The Hague. Europol is the European Law Enforcement Organisation, and its mission is to improve the effectiveness and cooperation of the competent authorities in the member states in preventing and combating terrorism, unlawful drug trafficking and other forms of serious international organised crime. It started limited operations in 1994 in the form of the Europol Drugs Unit (EDU), and has gradually had different criminal activities added to its responsibilities. However, Europol's birth was a difficult one, and it was only in 1999 that it really became a force to be reckoned with. The

current mandate of Europol includes the prevention and combating of
the following activities:

- illicit drug trafficking
- crimes involving illegal immigration networks
- illicit vehicle trafficking
- trafficking of human beings, including child pornography
- forgery
- illicit trafficking in radioactive and nuclear substances
- terrorism
- illegal money laundering.

Europol acts as a liaison body that collects, analyses and shares
intelligence in order to assist cross-border policing. It facilitates the
exchange of information through Europol liaison officers (ELOs),
seconded to Europol by member states as representatives of their
different national law enforcement agencies; provides operational
analysis in support of member states' operations; and provides expertise
and technical support for investigations and ongoing operations carried
out by the law enforcement agencies of the member states. Two case
studies — provided by Europol in interview — are indicative of the
work that it does. The first is called 'Operation Bravo', which, as the
result of close cooperation between several member States and Europol,
led to the largest drug seizure ever made in Finland, and the second
'Operation Samot', which resulted in the main suspect being arrested in
Britain in 1999.

Operation Bravo

Operation Bravo involved several months of close cooperation between
Dutch, German, Belgian, Spanish, Danish, Swedish, French and Finnish
law enforcement agencies and Europol to uncover a large-scale drug
trafficking organisation which had been operating throughout the EU for
several years. The organisation was also active outside of the EU,
particularly in the Russian Federation. The culmination of this cooperation was the arrest of 12 people in December 1999 in different
locations in Southern Finland, and the seizure of 179 kg of hashish, 21
kg of amphetamines, and 7 kg of marijuana. The alleged leader of this

particular drugs operation, from Kotka in Finland, had previously been convicted of an aggravated narcotics offence and is suspected of smuggling similar amounts of drugs into Finland on other occasions. Throughout Operation Bravo Europol acted as a coordinator of operational work, and the ELOs ensured that information and intelligence were exchanged.

Operation Samot

At the end of 1998, the Dutch law enforcement authorities started to investigate an Iraqi organised crime group which was trafficking foreign nationals to Scandinavia, Canada and the United Kingdom. The leading members of this group lived in The Netherlands, and initial results of the investigation revealed that the organisation was arranging several trips of illegal immigrants from The Netherlands via Belgium and France to the UK. To combat the group, Europol set up a cooperation network, and at the beginning of April 1999 an operational meeting was organised through the ELOs and intelligence shared between The Netherlands, Belgium, France and the UK. As a result, at the end of April the main target was arrested in England, with subsequent arrests taking place in The Netherlands and the UK.

While operations of this type are in the 'shop window' of Europol's work, the future operational role of the Organisation is still very much being developed against the backdrop of national concerns about the creation of a European 'superstate'. Some of these tensions (and how they will affect Europol) can be seen within the provisions of the Amsterdam Treaty. Article 30 of the Treaty suggests that the EU will promote police cooperation through Europol, first, by enabling it to facilitate and support the preparation, coordination and execution of investigations by competent authorities of member states, including operational actions of joint teams with representatives of Europol in a support capacity; secondly, by adopting measures allowing Europol to *ask* (emphasis added) the competent authorities to conduct and coordinate their investigations in specific cases; thirdly, by promoting liaison arrangements between prosecuting and investigating officials; and, lastly, by establishing a research, documentation and statistical network on cross-border crime. This does seem to suggest that Europol will shift from being simply an information and intelligence source to an organisation which is capable of instigating and coordinating investigations. However, in interview with the Deputy Director of Europol, David Valls-Russell — formerly of the Kent Constabulary — he admitted that some national police forces might not necessarily take a request from Europol seriously, and in this situation, perhaps in years to come, it might be necessary to change the word 'ask' (above) to 'instruct'. This raises the spectre of Europol becoming a European version of the FBI at some point in the future. Many will find this a step too far, but what cannot be doubted is that as crime becomes more global, our police will be required to embrace greater international cooperation.

CLOSER TO HOME

The need to establish a more European — and indeed international — outlook creates dilemmas. The system of laws, the machinery of criminal justice and the structure and governance of policing are very different in Britain from those in Europe. The European tradition is one where the law is more codified than in Britain, and European police forces generally lack the discretion and operational independence that characterise British policing. None of this presents an insurmountable barrier to greater information sharing, but it does raise questions which will need to be addressed before operational collaboration can be significantly extended. These questions are ultimately political and organisational, and they must not prevent us from dealing with more national and local concerns about our police, several of which we outlined in the Introduction. For whatever the need to establish greater cross-national cooperation, this should not be done at the expense of ignoring the needs of the local communities within which our police inevitably operate. Indeed, the 'intelligence' which is the lifeblood of Europol has to start in the houses, streets and boulevards of EU member states, and without that intelligence, policing — whether international or local — effectively grinds to a halt. So at the heart of these concerns is the question of whether or not our police are 'crime busters' or 'servants of the community'. Some might argue that they can be both at the same time — after all, 'busting crime' does perform a community service — but this argument seems to us to avoid the question. For 'crime busters' inevitably have to become armed and develop tactics which will distance the police from the community; 'crime busters' develop a culture of difference, rather graphically depicted in the dreadful popular policing book entitled *The Good Guys Wear Black*, which seeks to celebrate the specialised operational policing of confrontation and present this as our future — in effect as the only solution to rising crime. Yet as we have shown, it is the community which by and large provides the police with the intelligence to tackle crime, and without the community's support the police quite simply cannot function effectively.

It is this need to harness community support that we believe creates an agenda for the future of the police. To be servants of the community is no easy task. For, first, the police have to recognise that there is a variety of 'communities', each of which might equally want to be protected from crime and criminals, but which might nonetheless still see the police as representing a culture which is alien to them. This puts a great deal of pressure on the police to ensure that they recruit staff from ethnic minorities, both sexes and of different sexualities. While it is undoubtedly true that great steps are being taken by the police to recruit staff from these backgrounds, this is not simply a matter of recruitment. Rather, it is also about changing institutional cultures so that staff can work more flexibly so as, for example, to be able to accommodate their domestic needs or religious beliefs. For after recruitment has taken place the police also have to ensure that staff are retained, and that there is equity in promotion. If this is achieved then the police will truly be representative of the community, and this in turn will make their task easier.

From our research in Doncaster it is also clear that the public want the police to be more visible, and to be closer to them. This does not necessarily mean 'swamping' an area with police for a short period of time, or that there should be 'more Bobbies of the beat'. Rather, in the same way that shining a light on a customer's bedroom window late at night was a way that Household Security could demonstrate that it was providing a real and bespoke policing service to the community, so too our police have to move beyond trying to prove their worth through policing plans and key performance indicators and targets. All too often this simply seems like spin rather than substance, and ineffective spin at that. After all, how can a policing plan, boasting about a 3 per cent drop in burglaries or violent crime, which might get at most some local press coverage, hope to compete against the daily staple of sensational crime stories that dominate our broadcast and written media? Quite simply it cannot. The solution is not to give up, or to spend more on advertising successes, as useful as this in itself might be. Rather, the police need to convince people through their actions that they are doing their job; to find for themselves a 'torch on a bedroom window' so that they too can demonstrate their worth at the level where that message can have the most impact — in the community.

Lastly, the police will have to be accountable to that community. Despite a variety of initiatives in this area, local police authorities still seem to reflect the needs of white, middle class people, who are by no means representative of the local community as a whole. So too, the police have to maintain independence from greater political control, no matter how problematic this is becoming. Having a Home Secretary direct the police removes at a stroke any semblance of local accountability and control, and destroys — as was seen during the miners' strike — local support and authority. Perhaps it is here that the police face their greatest challenge. For faced with a vicious circle of sensationalist media reporting of violent crime, which breeds a disproportionate concern with violent crime and the sentencing of offenders, which in turn creates political pressure to 'do something' about crime, politicians inevitably respond with initiatives that serve little purpose other than ensuring their continued time in office. Expectations are heightened but rarely met, and in the end the police are left failing to satisfy either their political masters, or the community which they set out to serve. It does not need to be this way. Ultimately we believe that if local people — all local people — are provided with a service that meets their needs, by police whom they know and respect, and are given information about the true state of crime within their community, the police will be able to resist greater political encroachment and the temptation to turn them into versions of *Robocop*.

References

Alderson, J. (1979), *Policing Freedom* (Plymouth: Macdonald and Evans).

Association of Chief Police Officers (ACPO) (1995), Final Report of the Patrol Project Working Group (London: ACPO).

Audit Commission (1990), *Effective Policing: Performance Review in Police Forces* (London: HMSO).

Audit Commission (1993), *Helping with Enquiries* (London: Audit Commission).

Audit Commission (1996a), *Streetwise: Effective Police Patrol* (London: Audit Commission).

Audit Commission (1996b), *Tackling Crime Effectively* (London: Audit Commission).

Audit Commission (1996c), *Detecting Change: Progress in Tackling Crime* (London: Audit Commission).

Audit Commission (1999), *Annual Report on the Police and Fire Services* (London: Audit Commission).

Banton, M. (1964), *The Policeman in the Community* (London: Tavistock).

Bayley, D. H. (1996), 'What do the Police do?' in Sailsbury, Mott and Newbury, *Themes in Contemporary Policing* (London: Independent Committee of Inquiry into the Role and Responsibilities of the Police).

Blair, I. (1998), 'Where do the police fit in policing?' (paper delivered to ACPO summer conference, 16 July, unpublished).

Bottomley, K. and Pease, K. (1986), *Crime and Punishment: Interpreting the Data* (Milton Keynes: Open University Press).

Bowling, B. (1998), *The Rise and Fall of New York Murder*, Paper presented to the University of Cambridge/Police Research Group Seminar, 'Police and Crime Reduction', 3 March 1998.

Brogden, M., Jefferson, T. and Walklate, S. (1988), *Introducing Policework* (London: Unwin).

Burrows, J. and Tarling, R. (1982), *Clearing Up Crime* (London: HMSO).

Butler, R. A. (1962) speech to the ACPO Summer Conference, quoted in Oliver, I. (1987), *Police, Government and Accountability* (2nd edn) (London: Macmillan).

Clarke, R. and Hough, M. (1984), *Crime and Police Effectiveness* (London: Home Office Research Unit).

Coleman, C. and Moynihan, J. (1996), *Understanding Crime Data: Haunted by the Dark Figure* (Buckingham: Open University Press).

Critchley, T. A. (1978), *A History of Police in England and Wales* (London: Constable).

Cumming, E., Cumming, I. and Edell, L. (1964), 'The Policeman as philosopher, guide and friend', *Social Problems*, 12:3.

Davies, N. (1997), *Watching the detectives: how the police cheat in fight against crime*.

Davis, N. (1997), *Dark Heart* (London: Chatto & Windus).

Dixon, D. (1999), 'Police Investigative Procedures' in Walker, C. and Starmer, K. (eds), *Miscarriages of Justice: A Review of Justice in Error* (London: Blackstone Press).

Doncaster Metropolitan Borough Council, *Unitary Development Plan, Issues and Directory Report*, April 1990.

Emsley, C. (1991), *The English Police* (Harlow: Addison Wesley Longman).

Federal Bureau of Investigation (1994), *Crime in the United States — 1993* (Washington, DC: US Government Printing Office).

FitzGerald, M. (1999), *Searches in London under Section 1 of the Police and Criminal Evidence Act interim report of year one action programme* (London: Metropolitan Police Service).

Girling, E., Loader, I. and Sparks, R. (1998), 'Narratives of Decline: Youth Disorder and Community in an English Middletown', 38 *British Journal of Criminology* 388.

Hall, B. (1999), *Policing Europe: EU Justice and Home Affairs Co-operation* (London: Centre for European Reform).

Harker, L., (1996) *Poverty: The Facts* (London: Child Poverty Action).

Her Majesty's Chief Inspector of Constabulary (1994), *Annual Report 1993* (London: HMSO).

Her Majesty's Inspectorate of Constabulary (1998), *What Price Policing? A Study of Efficiency and Value for Money* (London: HMSO).

Her Majesty's Inspecorate of Constabulary (1999), *Winning the Race — Revisited* (London: HMSO).

Her Majesty's Inspectorate of Constabulary (2000), *On the Record* (London: HMSO).

Holdaway, S. (1983), *Inside the British Police* (Oxford: Basil Blackwell).

Home Office (1991), *Safer Committees* (London: HMSO).

Home Office (1993), *Police Reform: A Service for the Twenty First Century*, Cmnd 2281 (London: HMSO).

Home Office (1995), *Review of Police Core and Ancillary Tasks: Final Report* (London: HMSO).

Home Office Research and Statistics Department, 1995, Police Complaints and Discipline, *Statistical Bulletin 13/95* (London: Government Statistical Service).

Home Office Research and Statistics Department, 1998, 'The 1998 British Crime Survey', *Statistical Bulletin 21/98* (London: Home Office).

Home Office (1999), *Statistics on Race and the Criminal Justice System* (London: Home Office).

Hood, R. (1992), *Race and Sentencing: A Study in the Crown Court* (Oxford: Clarendon Press).

Jefferson, T. and Grimshaw, R. (1984), *Controlling the Constable: Police Accountability in England and Wales* (London: Muller).

Johnston, L. (1996), 'What is Vigilantism?', 36 *British Journal of Criminology* 220.

Joseph Rowntree Foundation (2000), *Poverty and Social Exclusion in Britain* (London: Joseph Rowntree Foundation).

Keegan, K. (1997), *Kevin Keegan — My Autobiography* (London: Little, Brown and Company).

Kelling, G., Pate, T., Dieckman, D. and Brown, C. (1974), *The Kansas City Preventative Patrol Experiment: A Summary Report* (Washington, DC: Police Foundation).

Kelling, G., Pate, T., Dieckman, D. and Brown, C. (1974), *The Kansas City Preventive Patrol Experiment: A Technical Report* (Washington, DC: Police Foundation).

Knight, S. (1983), 'The Brotherhood'. (London: Granada).

Leng, R. and Taylor, R. (1996), Blackstone's Guide to the Criminal Procedure & Investigations Act 1996 (London: Blackstone Press).

Lustgarten, L. (1986) The Governance of the Police (London: Sweet & Maxwell).

Macpherson, Sir W. (1999), The Stephen Lawrence Enquiry: Report of an Inquiry by Sir William Macpherson of Cluny, Cm 4262 (London: HMSO).

Mark, R. (1978), In the Office of Constable (London: Collins).

May, T. (1993), Social Research: Issues, Methods and Process (Buckingham: Open University Press).

McConville, et al (1991), The case for the prosecution: Police Suspects and the Construction of Criminality (London: Routledge).

Morgan, J. (1991), Safer Communities: The Local Delivery of Crime Prevention through the Partnership Approach (London: Home Office).

Morgan, R. and Newburn, T. (1997), The Future of Policing (Oxford: Clarendon Press).

Morrish, A. V. (ed.) (1987), Our Doncaster (Doncaster: Doncaster Library Service).

Morton, J. (1993), Bent Coppers (London: Little Brown).

Muncie, J. (1996), 'The Construction and Deconstruction of Crime' in Munci, J. and McLaughlin, E. (eds), The Problem of Crime (London: Sage).

Murray, C. (1984), Losing Ground: American Social Policy 1950–1980 (New York: Basic Books).

Newburn, T. (1995), Crime and Criminal Justice Policy (London: Longman).

Nicholas, R. M., Barr, R. J. and Mollan, R. A. B. (1993), 'Paramilitary punishment in Northern Ireland: A Macabre Irony', 34 The Journal of Trauma 90.

Oliver, I. (1987) Police, Government and Accountability (2nd edn) (London: Macmillan).

Police Complaints Authority (2001), Annual Report, 1999–2000 (London: PCA).

Police Foundation (1981), The Newark Foot Patrol Experiment (Washington, DC: Police Foundation).

Proceedings of Home Affairs Select Committee, 20.10.97, Hansard.

Punch, M. and Naylor, T. (1974), 'The Police and Social Service', 24 (554) *New Society* 358.

Rawlings, P. (1991), 'Creeping Privatization? The Police, the Conservative Government and Policing in the late 1980s', in Reiner, R. and Cross, M. (eds), *Beyond Law and Order: Criminal Justice Policy and Politics into the 1990s* (London: Macmillan).

Reiner, R. (1992a), *The Politics of the Police* (2nd edn) (Hemel Hampstead: Harvester Whestsheaf).

Reiner, R. (1992b) 'Codes, Courts and Constables: Police Powers since 1984', *Public Money and Management*, January–March 1992.

Reiner, R. (1994) 'Crime Control', *LSE Magazine*, Spring 6(1) 10.

Reiner, R. (1998), 'Policing Protest and Disorder in Britain' in Della Porta and Reiner, *Policing Protest* (Minneapolis: University of Minnesota Press).

Reiss, A. J. (1971), *The Police and the Public* (New Haven, Conn.: Yale University Press).

Reith, C. (1938), *The Police Idea* (Oxford: Oxford University Press).

Reith, C. (1943), *British Police and the Democratic Ideal* (Oxford: Oxford University).

Reith, C. (1948) *A Short History of the Police* (Oxford: Oxford University Press).

Renshaw, W. M. (1984), *An Ordinary Life: Memories of a Balby Childhood* (Doncaster: Doncaster Library Service).

Rose, D. (1997), *In the Name of the Law: The Collapse of Criminal Justice* (London: Vintage).

Scarman, Lord (1981) *The Brixton Disorders*, Cmnd 8427 (London: HMSO).

Sharp, D. and Wilson, D. (2000), '"Household Security": Private Policing and Vigilantism in Doncaster', May 39(2) *The Howard Journal of Criminal Justice* 113.

Sheehy Report (1993), *Report of the Inquiry into Police Responsibilities and Rewards* (Cm 2280) (London: HMSO)

Short, M. (1989), *Inside the Brotherhood* (London: Grafton).

Skolnick, J. (1966) *Justice without Trial* (New York: Wiley).

South, N. (1988), *Policing for Profit: The Private Security Sector* (London: Sage Publications).

Special Advisor to the Board of Police Commission (1992), *The City in Crisis: on the Civil Disorder in Los Angeles 21 October* (Los Angeles: Police Commission).

Spradley, J. (1979), *The Ethnographic Interview* (New York: Holt, Rinehart and Winston).

Storch, R. (1975), '"The Plague of Blue Locusts": Police Reform and Popular Resistance in Northern England, 1840–1857' XX *International Review of Social History* 61.

Thompson, W. and Mulholland, B. (1994), 'Paramilitary punishments and young people in West Belfast: Psychological effects and the implications for education', in Kennedy, L. (ed.), *Crime and Punishment in West Belfast* (Belfast: The Summer School).

Waddington, P. A. J. (1999), *Policing Citizens* (London: UCL Press).

Weaver, M. (1994), 'The New Science of Policing: Crime and the Birmingham Police Force, 1839–1842' 26 *Albion* 289.

Wilkins, G. and Hayward, P. (2001), *Operation of Certain Police Powers under PACE* (London: Home Office Statistical Bulletin).

Wilson, D. (1999), 'Delusions of Innocence' in Cullen, E. and Newell, T., *Murderers and Life Imprisonment* (Winchester: Waterside Press).

Wilson, D. and Ashton, J. (1998), *What Everyone in Britain Should Know About Crime and Punishment* (London: Blackstone Press).

Wilson, J. Q. and Kelling, G. (1982), 'Broken Windows', *Atlantic Monthly*, March 1982.

Yeo, H. and Budd, T. (2000), *Policing on the Public: Findings from the 1998 British Crime Survey* (London: Home Office Research, Development and Statistics Directorate).

Index